SPEAKING OUT, FIGHTING BACK

SPEAKING OUT, FIGHTING BACK

*Personal Experiences of Women
Who Survived Childhood Sexual
Abuse in the Home*

SISTER VERA GALLAGHER
With William F. Dodds

1985
MADRONA PUBLISHERS
SEATTLE

Published by
Madrona Publishers, Inc.
P.O. Box 22667
Seattle, WA 98122

Library of Congress
Cataloging-in-Publication Data

Gallagher, Vera.
Speaking out, fighting back.

Bibliography: p.
Includes index.
1. Child molesting—United States—Case studies.
2. Adult child abuse victims—United States—Attitudes.
3. Church work with women—United States—Catholic
Church. 4. Catholic Church—United States—Charities.
I. Dodds, William F. II. Title.
HQ72.U53G35   1985   362.7'044   85-15491
ISBN 0-88089-010-X

10 9 8 7 6 5 4 3 2 1

To the Good Shepherd Sisters
who have given 150 years of loving care
to girls and women throughout the world

Foreword

CHILDREN are being victimized at an alarming rate in this country. Paradoxically, that victimization often is at the hands of individuals with primary responsibility for protecting those children, their parents. Victimized children frequently suffer in silence—unaware of resources that could provide help, too young or too frightened to reach out for help, believing that the pain is their own fault.

According to statistics from the American Humane Association, the number of children reported to authorities as abused or neglected increased 123 percent between 1976 and 1982. Those are only the children reported, however. There is consensus that those reports are only the tip of the iceberg and that many more children are victimized, but receive no assistance.

We know that children who are victimized are at great risk to grow up and victimize other children. Victims become victimizers and each generation tragically inherits the pain of the previous generation. The scars of abuse and neglect include acute and chronic medical and emotional problems. Throughout childhood and adult years, victims often struggle with chronic depression, suicide attempts and other self-destructive behavior, chemical dependency, poor self-image, diminished ability to trust, nightmares, developmental delays, impaired interpersonal relationships, eating disorders, and problems with sexuality.

While the problems of abuse and neglect are probably as old as childhood itself, the willingness of society to intervene and interrupt the destructive cycle of abuse is relatively recent. Through efforts such as those of Sister Vera Gallagher, our awareness and determination to address the tragedy of abuse and neglect will increase and result in new hope for this and future generations of children.

FRED D. STRIDER, PH.D.
Nebraska Psychiatric Institute
University of Nebraska Medical Center

Preface

SINCE the mid-'70s, child welfare professionals have seen a steadily growing number of cases of children abused by some kind of sexual exploitation. In the late '70s, journalists, publishers, film and TV producers also discovered the problem.

Now the media are turning out books, magazine articles, TV programs, and newspaper accounts describing this alarming kind of abuse. Professionals are writing for their journals.

As a result, people at all levels, from politicians to the general public, are becoming aware of child sexual abuse.

How much of it occurs?

Masses of statistics have been accumulated over the past ten years, but the fact is that we don't really know the full extent.

This crime against children is, by its nature, secret. Typically, children and teenagers don't talk about it. But until we do talk about it, all of us, little will be done to prevent it from continuing or to repair the damage already done to so many innocent victims.

Of the variety of sex crimes against children, those perpetrated by relatives, persons known and loved by the children, are the most devastating, and the most difficult to resolve.

Can they ever be treated?

Yes. If, when the victim does speak out, we respond to the child (who may then be a teenager or adult) with unconditional love, respect, and support, that person can triumph. That statement is the thesis of my book.

To meet adults who have resolved their childhood victimization, or are in the process of doing so, I have traveled to Good Shepherd Sisters' programs throughout the country.

We Sisters would be the first to say that we have no special expertise in dealing with the victims of childhood sexual abuse in the home. Most often, as with professionals in general, we did not know whether the teens or women we served might have been sexually abused, and, in concert with the rest of society, did not ask.

Good Shepherd Sisters have a long history of working with exploited and oppressed women and children without regard for their religious faith or lack of it, treating them all with love and respect. I am very much aware of the valuable work being done by other professionals in both secular and religious settings, but for me, access to victimized women was far simpler through our Good Shepherd network. I knew that those women and children who had come in contact with the Sisters might trust me with their stories, simply because I am a Good Shepherd Sister.

I have treated both the stories and their narrators with reverence. My gratitude is extended, first of all, to the brave women in this book, each of whom has overcome.

My thanks go to Good Shepherd Sisters all over the country who have shared their homes and lives with me throughout this past year.

I acknowledge, also, my indebtedness to Eastern Airlines whose Get-Up-And-Go pass made possible my wide-ranging travel throughout the year and whose courteous employees offered me every service available.

I am grateful to Sister Patricia Maloney who first suggested this book and to Sister Barbara Beasley who provided the means of pursuing it.

I appreciate the time, expertise, and constructive criticism of the several readers of my manuscript: Dr. Fred Strider, Nebraska Psychiatric Institute; Rev. J. Moran, C.S.P., St. Patrick's Church, Seattle; Good Shepherd Sisters Barbara Beasley, Patricia Maloney, Pauline Bilbrough, and Victoria Andreoli.

The guidance and enthusiasm of Dan Levant, publisher, and Sara Levant, editor, combined to create a book which might otherwise have remained only a dream.

Finally, thanks to my co-author, Bill Dodds, for friendship, support, skill, and love; and to all on the staff of *The Progress*, Seattle, who cheered us on.

Contents

xiv

CONTENTS

Every incident and every story in this book is true. All personal accounts are taken directly from letters, tapes, and conversations with the author.

In every instance, the names, locations, and occupations of the victims of sexual abuse have been changed to preserve their privacy. All have given written permission to tell their stories. Locations of specific Good Shepherd Homes and the names of Good Shepherd Sisters have been changed to preserve the privacy of the victims and the confidentiality of their relationships with the Sisters.

SPEAKING OUT,
FIGHTING BACK

ONE

Rosemary

MY EARLY years were very happy; my parents were Italian immigrants, and my mother was a loving and caring person. We didn't have much money, but we were never hungry. A big family, each of us loved the others.

And then, suddenly, my mother died. My life felt like it was ended. I just wanted to die, too.

Because I was the oldest girl in our family, although I was only twelve, I became the mother, sort of. My father began getting very loving towards me. Then, one night, he took me to bed with him, and forced himself on me. He assured me that it was all right, and that's what dads and older daughters did. But it didn't feel right. So I suggested that we both go to our priest and talk to him about it. With that, he beat me, beat me the worst he ever beat, and my dad had always been strict about discipline, and had never spared the rod. With that, I knew it was wrong. But what could I do? I had to look after my little brothers; they had nobody else. If I told, what would happen to them?

So my dreadful existence went on until I was fifteen. Then I ran away; I wanted to talk to a social worker. I was put in juvenile detention. A woman introduced herself as my caseworker; sobbing, I told her the awful story.

My dad was arrested. They brought him to trial, and I had to be the witness. But before court, he came to see me. He said that if he went to jail, my little brothers would all be split up, and would all go to different orphanages. It would be the end of our family. So I lied in court; I took back everything I had said, and I told the court that I had made it up.

I despised myself and could not even look up. The judge and my caseworker knew that I had lied. One more shame, just added to the other.

My heart and soul were breaking. Everyone looked at me with scorn. I couldn't blame them. I longed for my mother; she would have known what to do. I felt unhappy and insecure. I put up a barrier around myself and crept into it like a turtle. I swore to myself never to let anybody hurt me again, nor to trust, nor even to like anyone again.

TWO

In Trouble

From my fifty years as a Good Shepherd Sister, I can remember hundreds and hundreds of the teenage girls with whom I have worked.

Never having attended a Catholic school, I knew nothing about Sisters. Just the same, when I was fifteen, I decided to join a religious order, and to do so at once, but my parents said that I could not go to a convent until I was seventeen.

Not long before I left, my mother gave me a booklet by a Franciscan priest, which was to provide my sex education. She said that after reading it I could ask her any questions I wished. The priest had written so vaguely, however, that I had no questions to ask, except that I wanted to know where babies came from, and how a woman could have a baby outside of marriage.

My mother explained that much.

Various pieces of literature came to me from the Good Shepherd Order, to which I had applied. (My mother had recommended the Order because she had known these Sisters in Ireland.) According to the brochures, the principal mission of the Sisters was to girls and women in trouble. Naturally I assumed that "in trouble" meant unmarried mothers.

During my first couple of months in the Convent I kept a sharp eye out for the babies I thought must be tucked away someplace. But, of course, there were no babies; Good Shepherd Sisters were devoted to other kinds of "in trouble."

My first year and a half with the Sisters was spent learning what the life was all about. I had hoped to devote the major part of my life to scripture-reading and prayer, but I quickly discovered that such would not be the case.

I learned, also, something about the "trouble" girls and women can get caught up in.

From our founding, Good Shepherd Sisters have been dedicated to helping girls and women with those kinds of problems which attract little popular sympathy: the adolescent coping with problems in the transition to adulthood, the uncared-for or unloved or unwanted, the prostitute, the prisoner, the drug and alcohol addict, the women drifters who are known as bag ladies, the don't-fits who have become today's psychiatric patients, and the innocent children growing up in morally dangerous circumstances. Good Shepherd Sisters work for and with all of these, without regard for religious affiliation.

During my second year with the Sisters in Vancouver, British Columbia, I spent a couple of hours a day with the girls and women in our care so that I could learn something about our mission. Most of them were older than I. My endeavor was to bring sunshine and love into their lives as I observed other Sisters trying to do.

I knew nothing, of course, about sexual abuse. That would come later.

Despite my naivete, I couldn't help noticing that Jeannie

had problems. She was twenty-two, perhaps, but she acted younger, and something about her chatter and laughter seemed forced. I had only the girls I had known in school to compare her with, but the stream of chatter and joking seemed strained and out of place. When I talked to Sister Agatha about this, she explained that Jeannie was coping with heavy problems because her own father had sexually abused her.

Never having heard of such a thing, I was shocked. I decided quickly that I would reach out to Jeannie with a special love and concern.

I saw Jeannie, along with the rest, for only one or two hours a day, for perhaps eight months. Then I was transferred to the States.

I never forgot Jeannie because I had been horrified at what she must have suffered, and I kept her in my prayers. My life quickly became so busy that I scarcely had time enough to write home. Just the same, I kept Jeannie in mind, even though I never expected to see or hear from her again.

Good Shepherd Sisters were cloistered at that time. Although not an order devoted primarily to prayer, we did value contemplation. When Sister Euphrasia started the Order in the mid-nineteenth century, it was believed that we could shut out the distractions of the "world" by living within a cloister. That meant that we did not leave our grounds except for education, medical and dental care, and emergencies. As we did not return home for visits, I had not gone back to my parents' home in Vancouver.

Following Vatican II, however, almost thirty years after I had left home, the bishops asked the Good Shepherd Sisters to get out into a needing world. Shortly afterward my father went into a hospital in Vancouver, seriously ill. My sister phoned me to come. I was then permitted to travel, but I could not get a plane out that night. I did have a flight booked for the next morning. Sadly for me, my father quietly slipped off during the night.

I was shattered by my father's death; I had loved him very much, and hadn't gone home since I was seventeen. It simply didn't seem possible that he was gone, and before I had time to say my last goodbye.

And then a letter came from Jeannie. The first woman sexually abused at home that I had ever known. How many years had passed since I had met Jeannie, since a time that seemed long, long ago? I was so deeply touched.

"I'm a nursing supervisor at the hospital your father died in," she wrote. "He talked about you, so I knew who he was. You couldn't come, so I took special care of him. I was on the floor the night he died. He passed away as he slept. I did anything and everything I could, and did it in your name.

"I waited these many years for an opportunity of thanking you. We met a long long time ago, many unhappy years ago, and we knew each other only briefly. But in you I sensed a special concern, a particular kind of caring love.

"Black days have come and gone. When the shadows seemed darkest I knew you were praying for me, and I remembered the radiance of your smile—a smile that has stretched over the intervening years.

"Exactly what you gave me so long ago, I don't really know. But it was special. I have always wanted to give you a token of gratitude which might be equally special. The opportunity finally came my way."

In this book I have chosen to recall those women, out

of the three thousand or so teenagers I have served, who I know were sexually abused at home.

I have wanted also to meet other women who had been sexually abused at home, and who had come into the radius of the caring love of the Sisters of the Good Shepherd. Accordingly, I have crisscrossed the country throughout this past year, meeting Good Shepherd Sisters and observing our various ministries to girls and women "in trouble."

Last fall I met Sister Kathleen in a women's emergency shelter assisting a middle-aged woman with a Ph. D. who had been living on the street. Like so many people on the streets she had been mentally ill, but would now be returning to her friends.

I sought out Sister Kathleen because she had worked with teenage girls for twenty-seven years. She keeps in touch with hundreds of them, now married or settled in various careers. In fact, Sister counted the contacts initiated by former girls, now women, in a recent six-month period. Within that six months, she received one thousand phone calls, letters, and personal visits.

Why do they phone, write and visit?

If a woman needs counseling, says Sister, or has experienced significant success, or completed a difficult educational course, she phones. "We are their extended family."

They might call or write about an error they've made, a new baby, to ask advice about a friend's problem, or a child's difficulty in school.

Or they might want to wish Sister a happy Christmas or Easter or whatever holiday, and reminisce about the old days.

"Some girls were placed with us for protection; some were

in conflict with family, school, or society; some had been sexually abused."

Sister remembers some sexually abused girls who were never again allowed to return home because they had reported the abuse.

"Girls who have been sexually abused in their own homes need extensive counseling; to my knowledge, they never completely recover from the trauma. It is most likely to show up when they try to form a close personal relationship, as in marriage.

"When the mother tells the daughter that she does not approve of the father's behavior, then the girl has a better chance. But if the mother continues living with the father, then the girl believes that the incest was excusable, and she has a hard time coping.

"The entire family needs counseling. But I've never known a daughter who could return home and live there with the father in the house. Perhaps it can be done, but I haven't seen it.

"Most of the girls I worked with had never committed an illegal act. Those who had run away from home often did so for self-protection. My work was primarily preventive."

Most of the girls eventually became wives and mothers. And then Sister Kathleen begins listing the kinds of careers those Good Shepherd girls chose: city and state police officers; nurses; beauticians; teachers; social workers; x-ray technicians, secretaries, accountants. She recalls a practicing attorney who had come to the Home after dropping out of high school for two years; she had gotten a new start in the Good Shepherd School. Sister Kathleen smiles to remember her one dog-catcher. She takes pride in the young woman who became a Protestant minister and phoned for assistance with her first funeral sermon; she is currently a chaplain in the armed forces. And she recalls the girl who started out cleaning houses, and now, with her husband, directs a big cleaning operation in a distant state.

I have talked to Vicki Wagner, director of the Orion Center in Seattle, a facility ministering specifically to one of America's latest phenomena: the street kids. "Most of the street kids we see have been sexually abused," Vicki told me, "and last year we saw 477 of them."

Benedictine Sister Bernie Ternes is well known on the Seattle streets. For some years Sister Bernie worked at the Monroe, Washington, men's correctional facility, for many more years, at the Church Council's shelter for up to 200 homeless people, mostly men, in Seattle. Sister is now working at Seattle's Martin de Porres shelter for 100 homeless men.

"Were many of your transient men sexually abused as children?" I asked her.

"Oh, yes. The greatest percentage of men on the streets here," said Sister. "That's what ruined their lives. The sexual abuse caused permanent harm by making them feel guilty and depriving them of self-respect. They end up in correctional facilities, and finally gravitate to the streets."

I remember talking with Norm Riggins, director of Nightwatch, Seattle, and an ordained minister of the Evangelical Church of North America. "I watch the kids hustling on the streets," he told me, "selling their bodies because they have no other commodity to sell. Almost 100 percent of them were sexually abused, most of them at home."

I had joined the Good Shepherd Order with the primary objective of seeking contemplation: the light of God, the love, the silence, the peace. I did not want to teach teenagers, some of whom were emotionally and behaviorally handicapped: it was too hard, too draining, too demanding. Just too. . . .

I got dragged into the work, really. Confronted with children's pain, I had reluctantly shuffled onwards. Having come for prayer, I had stayed to get involved in the Good Shepherd mission to teenage girls in trouble.

But I did want to quit, often. Sometimes all over again, every day.

The teenagers we Sisters served throughout my years of working with them were often referred to by the public as "juvenile delinquents." In my opinion, they were not "delinquent"—they were victims.

Victims burdened by others' sins.

Exactly how many of the teens I served had been sexually abused at home, I don't really know. Until recently nobody talked about sexual abuse. Even today, children and teenagers very seldom reveal the sexual abuse by which they were victimized at home.

Although I knew that the majority of teenagers I worked with had been physically abused, I usually did not learn of the sexual abuse until after they had left the Good Shepherd Home. Generally, many years had intervened before a girl, now a successful woman, began writing, phoning, and coming back to tell me the rest of the story and to ask for my help. In conformity with society's conventions, they had kept their own secret.

Keeping the secret—not knowing, not seeing—is an easier path for all of us. If I were to walk that path again, I wonder whether I'd keep my eyes half-shut, making sure that I could not see.

Robert Frost said he chose the road less traveled by. Less traveled highways tend to be filled with potholes and dead ends; they end up in undesirable locations. Personally, I would have preferred to keep to the main highway: more sterile, but safe. And with so many people on it that, by sheer force of numbers, they shroud the scenery. I don't have to see the violated children along the freeway, and I don't pick up hitchhikers. Going where everybody else goes helps keep the secret. Most of us follow that route simply because everybody else takes it.

I like to keep my mouth shut about bad news, remembering the prophet Jeremiah groaning at the bottom of his dark pit. His fellow citizens threw him there, out of sight and hearing, because he brought them so much bad news. I'm scared of that cold dank pit. I'd rather not tell gloomy tales, another reason why I'd rather keep that secret.

I like a calm atmosphere. Phones and doorbells shatter tranquility. They intrude on my life; I don't know why we ever allowed them to be invented.

That also accounts for my reluctance to shatter your peace with these stories of girls and women breaking their silence. You'll be angry, I'm afraid.

When I read Alexandr Solzhenitsyn's *Gulag Archipelago,*

one passage reached out to me: "In keeping silent about evil, in burying it deep within us so that it appears nowhere on the surface, we are implanting it, and it will rise up a thousandfold in the future."

I can't keep silent any longer.

I wish I could, but I can't.

Some women have asked me to tell their stories.

I have asked other women for their permission to write the stories they have shared with me.

With these stories, I'm shattering the secrecy and the silence. I'm providing these girls and women with a platform from which to speak out, and in so doing, fight back.

THREE

Marcie

OUR HOME was strict, and I do mean strict. We belonged to the Church of God of Prophecy, Worldwide, and my dad saw to it that we did what we were supposed to.

We never called our parents Mom and Dad. It was "Yes, Ma'am," and "No, Sir." We never talked about feelings, and we never, never discussed sex. We were ordered never to talk outside of the family about anything that happened in the family.

My dad used his belt, and he used it freely. Any one of us children getting out of line could expect a whipping. My father and my brother John did not get along at all. Their relationship was terrible.

My brother John began taking me into a closet and touching my breasts and other private parts. He started when I was about nine years old. He didn't hurt me, but I did not know what to do. I hated it, but I couldn't stop him. He was bigger than me, and I couldn't tell.

Telling would mean a hard whipping for both of us. Whippings hurt, and I didn't want another one when I had done nothing to deserve it. It bothered me, but I had nobody to talk to. After all, we had been warned, within an inch of our lives, that we *never* talked about anything in the family *outside* of the family.

My brother's liberties continued until I was about twelve, and in the seventh grade. My parents had moved to another house in a big city, they and we six children. My father got injured in a car accident and suffered head injuries. When he came home after hospitalization and therapy, he had changed. Always stern, he now displayed a lot of anger, too. He didn't beat us daily, but he beat all of us a lot. Even so, I loved him very much. I have always loved my father. I sensed a confusion of undercurrents in our home, but was too young and too naive to sort them out.

My father caught my brother and me in my bedroom. Very angry, he hollered and hollered at my brother. In any case, their relationship was always bad, as I have said. John had not really hurt me, but my father whipped him and whipped him hard. Then he jerked me out of the closet, dragged me to the front room, and yelled, "I'll show you!"

I expected a whipping. My father told me to take off my clothes and lie down on the sofa. Then, with my brother in the room, he took off all his clothes. At this point, I didn't understand what sex is: we were never allowed to discuss sex in any way; when my periods started, I thought I was dying. Now, in a blazing fury of anger, my father forced intercourse with me. It hurt, physically, a lot. Then he said, "Now you know."

I thought, "I don't know anything." And I hated him. Oh, how I hated him!

We were never allowed to talk back, so I went to my room and sobbed. From the depths of anger and despair, I asked God why he even made me. God, like everybody else, didn't answer.

My brother John still didn't quit. To me it was incredible, but he didn't quit, and he was stronger than I. And, after what my dad had done to me, I certainly couldn't tell.

Once, when my parents were gone as well as my oldest brother and sister, John came into my room after I had gone to bed. "Get out!" I said.

He wanted to get into bed with me, but I would not allow that. He masturbated and left. I wanted to find something big and heavy and throw it.

I considered myself the protector of my baby sister. When I came home one day, she was crying. "What's wrong?"

"I can't tell you."

"Oh, yes, you can," I said with a sinking heart. "What happened?"

John had forced himself on her.

I tried to comfort her as best I could. I ached for somebody to talk to. We both needed help, but I did not know what to do.

My brother ran away at that point; went through several foster homes, and then jail. He never came home again except to steal. But the damage was done. The damage is done the very first time.

My oldest sister married; my oldest brother joined the service. I was left at home with the two younger ones.

If my mother was home when I returned from school, she was in the bedroom with another woman. I thought perhaps they were sorting rummage, or doing embroidery together. But the time spent by my mother and another woman in the bedroom got longer and longer. Something *had* to be wrong.

I still had been given no sex information whatever.

My father came back to visit us—our parents had separated—and I told him about mother and her women friends. He tried to explain to me what was going on, but I couldn't believe it. How could I? She was my mother. Anyhow, my head was on overload; I could not absorb one more fact. So much was going on that I could not think, and I could not face the truth.

That summer my father took us children to a distant city to our church's state convention. We had a wonderful time, free of anger and abuse. When we got back to the house it was empty. I fell and sprained my ankle, so my dad took me to the hospital emergency room.

There we learned that my mother was in that same hospital. She asked me to bring her rollers and hairpins. My ankle hurt, but I hobbled about the house and got them.

A woman was in my mother's room, a big tall woman. I distrusted her immediately, took an instant dislike to her.

The woman invited us three children out to get some pop. It was hot and we were thirsty, so we agreed. She took us out the back way, into a waiting police car.

The police car took us to the juvenile detention center.

Never, not ever, will I forget what happened. Nobody explained anything either to me or to the two younger ones. We had never done anything wrong. I had no idea why we were in a police car or in a detention center, and nobody there made any effort to explain anything.

The three of us were taken to a foster home, and dumped off. The foster mother had three other girls living there. "Why am I here?" I asked. No reply.

Next day the police officer came back and said she was my caseworker. I knew a bit about caseworkers because my brother had had caseworkers. She said that during the weekend my mother had reported that my father had raped me. "He did not," I said, having not the slightest idea of what "rape" meant. She treated us like three delinquents.

I was thirteen years old and the one who took care of

my young brother and sister all summer. Then we went back home.

"Why doesn't Dad come back?" I asked.

"You'll understand later," said my mother.

But I didn't want to understand later, I wanted to understand *now*.

I had loved my parents, but I was beginning to dislike my mother. She acted as though I were the mother of the two little ones, and expected me to take care of them.

My little brother wanted to bring his new coat to school one day for show and tell. I was sick in bed with a cold. Mother was still in bed, too lazy to get up. She ordered me to get him off to school.

"You can wear your new coat," I said.

"He cannot," countermanded my mother.

Suddenly I was angry, white-hot angry. I got that coat and gave it to my brother. "Wear it," I said. And I hugged him. I will never forget how happy he was about that coat.

My mother came down and whipped me for letting him take his new coat. I had never answered back before, but now I was furious. "Who do you think you are?" I yelled. "You don't take care of him, I do."

"Don't talk to me like that, I'll knock your teeth out!"

"Go ahead," I answered.

She did, and she pretty nearly did knock them out. I wanted to run away, but I couldn't leave my little brother and sister. My mother went off to one of her women friend's house. "Don't come back," I yelled after her.

The little ones returned. I bathed them, gave them dinner, and we played games and watched TV, and had fun.

My mother came in and yelled at me for not washing the clothes.

I was still sick the next day, but went to school anyway. It was easier than staying home. At the last period I was called to the counselor's office. There sat that same caseworker. "What are you doing here?" I demanded. "I haven't done anything wrong."

"We've come to take you."

"Take me where?"

No answer.

Again, in a police car, without even letting me get my coat and hat, they drove me to the juvenile detention center. They would not let me phone anybody. My father came that evening, but they would not let him in.

Admissions procedure stripped me of whatever dignity I might have had left.

I had to take off all my clothes in front of that matron, take a shower before her, allow her to check all the openings in my body for drugs.

I said, "I've never done anything; I've never touched drugs." Useless.

I was locked alone in a room for twenty-four hours.

I stayed in that detention center for a month or six weeks before I was sent to the Good Shepherd Hom   All kinds of court hearings intervened before the final decision was made.

I hated the thought of the Good Shepherd Home, but was relieved that I was going *someplace*.

Looking back now, I realize that I was just beginning to recognize my angers, hatreds, bittersweet relationships with my parents, and just starting to get courage enough to talk. I hated my caseworker, but at least I could talk, and she didn't tell me to shut up.

While in the detention center I discovered, with a shock, that I was not the only abused girl. Other girls had had fathers and brothers and various relatives take them to bed, too. I also discovered that I was one naive little girl. I was given the most extensive sex education ever compressed into six weeks, all of it in street talk. In the first three days, in fact, I had learned the whole lot. I was shocked to nausea, and I was scared. Living with all those girls with serious problems frightened me. I had never committed a crime.

FOUR

Until We Speak Out

SADLY, both girls and boys are all too often subjected to sexual assaults in their own families. This fact has been repeatedly unearthed in the past century, and as repeatedly buried. One cannot explore in depth the emotional and sexual lives of women without discovering, among some of them, the incest secret. Those investigators who unearth it have, until recently, often pretended they never saw it. The facts are simply too horrifying for most of us to absorb.

A pall of secrecy hangs over the sexual abuse of children within their own homes. This kind of abuse may take many forms: exhibitionism, fondling, photography, sadism, incest between father and daughter or son; between natural father, adoptive father, foster father, stepfather, or mother's boyfriend and daughter or son. It may occur between mother and child; among uncles and cousins and relatives; or between brother and sister, especially when the two are not really related, as with stepchildren or in a foster family.

At this time in history, child sexual abuse has exploded into public consciousness, not necessarily because it has increased, but because the issue has been championed by two powerful coalitions: the feminist movement and the children's protection movement. Both of these groups have had experience pushing social policy and know how to dramatize issues.

Besides, we now realize that childhood sexual abuse is a different kind of problem than we had once supposed: we now know that a great deal of sexual abuse takes place in the home and is perpetrated by relatives, especially fathers and stepfathers.

We have realized, further, that most victims never tell, and that the assault is psychologically damaging.

A careful study conducted in 1978 of 930 San Francisco women, using fourteen questions instead of only one broadly based question, found that 38 percent of these women had been sexually assaulted by age seventeen. Diana Russell, director of this study, also reported that one out of six women who had a stepfather as a principal figure in her childhood was sexually abused by him, compared to a rate of one out of forty abused by biological fathers.

Grandfather-granddaughter incest is reported to account for 10 percent of all reported cases of childhood sexual abuse in the family.

According to Dr. J. Conte, University of Chicago, 47 percent of sexual abusers are members of children's own families, with an additional 40 percent being known by the children; in only 8 to 10 percent of the cases are the abusers strangers.

These figures would suggest that at least three million American women may be suffering from the long-term effects of earlier sexual abuse by fathers, stepfathers or other male relatives.

Dr. David Finkelhor of the University of New Hampshire points out that if no more than 10 percent of all girls and 2 percent of all boys were sexually abused, that would total 210,000 children under the age of eighteen each year.

Psychologist Henry Giarretto, founder of the Child Sexual Abuse Treatment Program in Santa Clara, California, estimates that more than 250,000 children in this country are molested in their homes each year. In light of the data which we have, however, it appears that both of these projections are too low.

The consequences of incest are devastating. Dr. Judith Herman of Harvard found, in her study of incest victims, that 38 percent had attempted to kill themselves.

Of 437 adolescent girls admitted to one psychiatric hospital for emotional problems, 61 reported an incestuous involvement, with the average age of the first incident being eleven years old.

Nationally, in 1982, the latest date for which we have the figures, the Center for Disease Control in Atlanta reported 10,453 children fourteen and under had contracted gonorrhea; of these 2,100 were under ten years of age. An additional 238 children, fourteen and under, had syphilis, a more serious venereal disease.

Dr. Gene Abel, a psychiatrist at the Sexual Behavior Clinic at New York State Psychiatric Institute, points out that 44 percent of all incest offenders have molested other children, and that 18 percent admit to forcible rape.

According to Dr. Jean Holroyd of the University of California at Los Angeles, 5½ percent of the 1000 therapists she studied engaged in sexual relations with their patients. Since May, 1985, the malpractice insurance policy of the American Psychiatric Association no longer covers sexual misconduct.

Cultural barriers have long been erected against incest, and primitive tribes often enforce strict taboos against it. When incest is considered to be a sin, and a very serious sin, it becomes closely guarded as a family secret.

More than that. Most of us experience such revulsion over the possibility of a parent abusing a child for that parent's selfish pleasure that we don't want to hear or know anything about it at all. For one thing, all of us are fragile, all hold our treasure in earthen vessels, and all of us know in our secret depths that we could do likewise. The news of another person's crime hammers away at our own restraining walls, terrifying us.

Denying that sexual abuse within a family could take place, or could have occurred in a family we know, or could be happening in our neighborhood, helps each of us to maintain our own integrity. It enables us also to continue to believe in the basic goodness of humanity; we've got to trust people we live with or live in fear.

Because of such strong feelings, society at large chooses to ignore incest, deny it. Unfortunately, while society protects its own feelings and shuts its eyes tight against the shame, children are being devoured.

Who is that "society?" You and I, judges, physicians, lawyers, social workers, ministers, teachers, police officers, mothers and fathers, religious personnel. Churches want to hear of incest no more than the police; want to believe that none of *their* members could conceivably commit such an offense; want to hope that they have saved the unregenerate; want to believe that they have protected the weak; want, in short, to deny any possibility of incest among their own members. All these people in the helping professions assist the perpetrators of incest by guarding their guilty secret.

Sister Helen, who has worked in child care in five Good Shepherd residential treatment centers, told me that most of the teens she worked with had been sexually abused. Then, as a pastoral counselor, she worked with adult sex offenders committed for treatment to a closed psychiatric setting.

"I found," she says, "that most of the adult sex offenders had been sexually abused in childhood, too. In fact, as far as suffering goes, they suffered no less than their victims.

"Again and again one of the men would say to me, 'I don't know why I am telling you this; I never told anybody before,' and then the history of childhood sexual abuse poured out.

"The problem is the secrecy. The more totally and the longer that childhood abuse is buried and secret, the more powerfully it influences behavior.

"We must break the barrier.

"For the sake of the children, we must learn how to talk about sexual abuse—and that includes all of us."

Even police officers need special training in the area of child sexual abuse because their own intense feelings of anger at the offender, and what he or she has done to the child, can interfere with an officer's objective investigation of a case. They may, as a result, obtain evidence illegally, or it may be incomplete, with the result that the case is thrown out of court.

Psychiatrists, too, can help guard the secret.

Sigmund Freud, the patriarch of modern psychoanalysis, stumbled onto the secret of incest early in his career. Searching for the cause of hysteria, he gained the trust and confidence of many women patients. They told him about incestuous relationships with male relatives who were, as Freud knew, outwardly conventional, prosperous, and well-behaved. At first he believed the women, but he became increasingly uncomfortable with what these disclosures told him about respectable family men. If what these women said was true, then incest was not an offense relegated to the poor and the criminal members of society, but a fact of life in the established respectable patriarchal family.

Freud might have published his findings and lived with them, but his belief that hysteria was often caused by incest in early life was rejected by the establishment of his time, and his own reputation and work might have been imperiled. Psychoanalyst Alice Miller writes:

> Sometimes I have to ask myself how many children's corpses psychoanalysts require as proof before they will stop ignoring their patients' childhood suffering or trying to talk them out of it with the aid of the drive theory. . . . It is unlikely that analysts will be able to alter the incidence of child abuse, but as long as they go on espousing theories that can be used to deny and cover up flagrant mistreatment, they will prevent their patients as well as the general public from becoming conscious of the truth.

She says that because some colleagues had responded to her ideas with "embarrassment, indignation, resentment, open rejection, or anxiety," she was able to understand the social reaction back in Freud's time which led to his denial of actual sex abuse, and his promotion of the Oedipal theory.

Freud took the easier way out, and announced that his patients longed for and therefore fantasized sexual encounters with fathers and male relatives. Blaming the women was easier than believing them.

Freud traced a seductive path of denial which has been well

trodden ever since, and which has guarded the secret. In fact, as recently as 1975, one textbook on basic psychiatry stated that in only one case out of a million does incest actually occur.

When I was principal of one Good Shepherd school in the midwest in the early '30s, a child was placed there who showed severe behavior problems. We did not have then, as we do now, a staff psychiatrist and a psychologist. The girl's caseworker requested a psychiatric conference to provide direction for her treatment.

All of us involved with her assembled with the psychiatrist. He directed questions to each of us. Then he declared that the tenor of the girl's life was being severely disrupted by her fantasies of a sexual relationship with her father. He asked that one Sister, of whom the girl was especially fond, sit by her bed as she was falling asleep at night and allow her to share her fantasies. Once talked out, he said, they would exercise less power over her behavior.

The suggestion was not followed exactly, but the Sister did encourage the girl to talk to her. She found that the child had been sexually abused by her father.

Children subjected to incest usually guard the secret with more fervor than anybody else except the perpetrator.

The reasons for the victim's secrecy are legion.

Incest usually begins before puberty and often continues until the victim is old enough to run away. The grandfather, or father, or other close relative does not need to use force; this person is already trusted by the child. He may ask the girl to keep the matter secret between the two of them because it is a very special relationship, and then purchase her cooperation by buying her gifts. One thirteen-year-old girl whose adoptive father initiated sex when she was six years old, told me that he asked her to keep the matter a secret because he would have to go to jail if she told anyone. In return, he offered to buy her anything she wanted, and he did. The three natural children and two adopted children referred to in the next chapter were told by the father who abused them that if they ever mentioned the fact to anybody, he would personally kill the child and the mother. The children were so frightened that not one of them knew that the father was abusing the other children in the family at the same time.

Some years ago, two sisters were brought to a Good Shepherd Home at which I was the principal. The problem presented was the refusal of the younger girl to speak. She had suddenly stopped talking, and either nobody in the family knew why, or they were not saying. At that time, in a separate building, we cared for children placed with us for protective custody.

Lucy was in grade seven. She did her lessons and kept up with her schoolwork, but she did not speak. She played games with the other children, each of whom was making it her goal to get Lucy talking, but she never said a word. She played volley ball and baseball, but never a sound escaped her lips.

After one year, Lucy's caseworker began making plans to take Lucy home. Certainly, we had not helped her to speak. *Then* Lucy talked: she was frightened into speech.

Lucy's mother had several children and she worked long and hard to support them. As a result, she was away from home most of the time. One day Lucy's father came home and forced himself on the child. Then he warned her that if she ever told, he would kill her mother. Lucy tried so hard not to tell that she wouldn't speak another word. She did tell now, only because she was afraid that if she went home her father would come back.

Lucy and her sister did not go back home; Lucy remained at the Home until her graduation. In fact, she never went home again.

In another case, two teenagers told me that when they questioned their father about the rightness of his actions, he whipped them unmercifully. Young children, unable to live on their own, guard the secret because they are bought with gifts, threatened, or beaten into submission.

Children have other compelling reasons for secrecy: they fear that nobody will believe them, or that they will be blamed; they feel guilty, thinking they must have done something wrong to bring about this violation of their persons; or they may genuinely love those fathers who are otherwise good and kind to them, and willingly submit. They may even become addicted to sex, and therefore want it to continue.

A teenager, while placed in our care, had two brief psychotic episodes. Both times I took her to a psychiatrist who had been recommended to me, and she was temporarily hospitalized. After the second episode I asked her caseworker to try something else: the girl was clearly more victim than delinquent. Years later she began writing and phoning me. At that time she was an adult probation officer in an eastern state.

She needed counseling or help of some sort, she told me. Her own father had sexually abused her before she came to the Good Shepherd; her foster father did so after she left us.

"And," she said, "I've never told anybody, but when you brought me to say goodbye to that psychiatrist, he kissed me, and it was *not* a fatherly kiss."

"Sally!" I exclaimed, "why didn't you tell me? You knew other girls were seeing him."

"Yes," she said, "but I didn't think anybody would believe me." In other words, the psychiatrist was a professional with a good reputation, and Sally was a disturbed young person.

A teenager who tells her mother about the sexual liberties taken by her father may be slapped and told, "Shut up, you little bitch! You led your father on," as more than one girl has told me. The fact that the father has turned to the daughter makes the girl a competitor with the mother. If the marriage is already shaky, the mother does not know how to handle the situation.

When a thirteen-year-old girl told me that her adoptive father had begun abusing her when she was eight, I asked, "Why didn't you tell your mother?"

"Because," said the child, "we didn't get along. She was always accusing me of lying. I knew she would say that this was just a bigger lie than the rest." In cases of incest, the girl's relationship with the mother is a crucial factor which can contribute to the shroud of secrecy.

Sometimes the child does not tell because she really loves her father and treasures their relationship.

Sister Beatrice told me of a girl placed in a Good Shepherd Home in which she was then a child-care worker. She was a lovely girl, Beatrice said, with a delightful disposition. She was also very pretty. Her father initiated sexual relations with her when she was three years old, and had continued the sexual relationship for years. When she was fifteen he had suddenly left the home. Beatrice thinks he probably did so in an attempt to break his obsession with that one daughter. Meanwhile, the teenager was placed in the Good Shepherd Home for protective custody. When the father returned home he went berserk one day, shot his wife and two of his other children, and was gunning for a third when the little boy said, "Are you going to kill us all, Daddy?" He threw the gun away. Beatrice believes he intended to shoot them all and then himself, half-crazed because of his inability to break his obsession with his daughter.

He was given the death sentence. Sister Beatrice brought the daughter to see her father in prison before he was executed. The girl eventually married and had a family, and that family "is probably the backbone of her parish," said Beatrice. Because of the father's gentleness and love, the girl seems not to have been harmed by the incest.

That kind of case is rare but it does happen. Then the child keeps the secret because she values the relationship.

Children may also keep the secret because they become addicted to sex. I recall, when I was an intake worker in a Home in the midwest, reviewing an application for the admission of two girls, both of whom had been sexually abused by their father. The children liked the experience so much that they were inserting any round smooth object such as skipping rope handles into themselves while they were held for detention for testing and screening. Such children tend, later on, to become promiscuous and run away from home.

Another reason for the child to keep the matter a secret lies in the long and difficult judicial procedure. Marilyn's children, described in the next chapter, had to repeat their story fifteen times to different legal and judicial representatives, mostly men. Few children are resilient enough to cope with that kind of ordeal.

The entire family has powerful reasons for keeping family sexual abuse a secret.

In the first place, the father or other perpetrator will probably go to jail; at the least, he will have to move out of the family home. That leaves the mother with the financial burden of providing for the children. Should some of the children be too young for her to leave alone, she can't get a job. Existing on Aid to Dependent Children is precarious because the money provided is usually insufficient.

The mother is also bereft of marital sex and has to cope with her own sexual needs. Moreover, she is forced to raise the children alone.

One alternative is for the child to be moved into a foster home while the marriage is maintained intact. The mother may choose not to believe the child so that her husband stays with her. When this happens, the child views being taken out of her home as punishment for her behavior; her own guilt feelings are thus heightened.

Currently, with so much appearing in the popular press about sexual abuse, children may already understand or have learned from a schoolmate's experience that disclosure will mean being taken away from home. The secrecy is further reinforced.

Worse yet, the whole family is disgraced in the eyes of their community. Children are ashamed to continue in their own schools; the family is embarrassed to go to church or to social functions. The community itself might like to offer support but is too shocked to know how to do it effectively. Society wants to keep the secret as much as the family and we who are that society convey that message.

Supposing the father gets a prison sentence, he may leave threatening to even the score with the child who revealed the secret when he gets out. In prison he will get no help. When he is again turned loose on society, he may indeed return to the family to get even. One woman, whose husband was one of those who went to prison, told me, "He could come back and shoot us all, I do realize that. In fact, when you read of a man killing his wife and all the children and then shooting himself, I'm sure the hidden factor in those cases is incest.

"We learn to live with it."

Families of sex abusers show several characteristics, although, of course, not all families with this kind of profile harbor a sex abuser.

Families in which incest occurs are "closed" entities. Children are warned, and have been told since their earliest years, that nothing which happens within that family is to be talked of outside. Relationships with neighboring families and with the community at large are distant; the closed family celebrates and mourns by itself.

One child of ten, for instance, later placed in a Good Shepherd Home for protective custody, had been rented out by her mother to various men with whom she slept for maybe months at a time; the same procedure was followed with her sisters. The girl did not know that this arrangement was unusual. She had not discussed it outside of her family. She thought all girl-children slept with strangers and then went off to school while the men went off to work.

Families in which the father sexually abuses a child are often patriarchal in structure. The father is seen as a strong figure who makes all the decisions, parcels out punishments and rewards, and provides for the family. The father is outwardly a rigidly "good" man, often quite religious, and he may be eminently respectable. That combination of characteristics is one of the reasons for Freud's disavowal of his own findings.

Children in families with incest are often neglected; neither mother nor father makes it a priority to know where the child is nor what she or he might be doing. I've seen this myself. For eleven years I was engaged in parish ministry in Seattle. Usually, I did not drive home until after 10:00 P.M. or later. I was amazed to see the number of children, five and six years old, who were playing alone on city streets during the summer months. The potential for physical or sexual abuse was obvious.

One Good Shepherd Sister told me of a child of eight who arrived in school with more money than her family could possibly afford to give her. It turned out that she had been prostituting on the streets after school, not getting home until 10:30 or 11:00 P.M. Her mother had not questioned the youngster as to where she spent the intervening hours.

Often parents in such families are so burdened by their own problems that they cannot direct their attention to the children.

This kind of family may engage babysitters without careful regard to their qualifications. Too often, Mom's current boyfriend indulges in sex with the youngsters. One girl told me that her stepgranddad initiated sex with her when she was six years old; her mother and stepfather dropped her off at granddad's every weekend for the entire weekend.

"Did you tell your mother?" I asked.

She shook her head. "I told my stepsister. Granddad had

done the same to her. She said that if I told anybody, my mother would be terribly hurt and Granddad would have to go to jail and the family would be disgraced. So I never told."

Later on, the mother divorced this particular stepfather. The child was free of the stepgranddad. And then Mom's boyfriend sexually abused her. "I took off," she said. "What was the use of talking?"

She "took off" at the age of eleven.

Often, in cases of incest, the marriage is deteriorating. The parents may have ceased communicating, or the mother may have died, or the mother may have begun "retiring" from life and leaving the home duties to the oldest girl, including sexual duties. In this situation, the mother is glad to be relieved of the burden, becoming a willing cooperator in the abuse.

If the mother is dead it might be assumed that the father has turned to the oldest girl for sex because he could not get his satisfaction elsewhere. That supposition is absurd. A man can satisfy his needs in a multitude of ways other than turning to his own daughter. Studies indicate that those men who commit incest are sexually attracted to children.

In cases of sadistic behavior, the father needs a willing accomplice for his ugly physical abuse; or, if the mother is the abuser, she needs a cooperative helper. Should the family have only one parent, then that abusive mother or father must win the cooperation of other children in the family. If the parent exhibits violent behavior but confines it to one child, the other children are relieved to be spared the beatings, etc., and may help keep the secret.

According to Rev. James Royce, S.J., founder of the nationally known alcohol studies program at Seattle University, in 80 to 90 percent of cases of incest, the abuser is under the influence of alcohol. Those families in which one or both parents are alcoholics are, again, at risk for child sexual abuse.

Families with histories of violence may also be sexually abusive for children. Husbands who batter wives typically abuse their children, sexually or physically, or both.

The mother who was abused as a child or teenager may want to protect her children from abuse but does not know how. Because she never received protection herself, she has no maternal role model which she might copy. Furthermore, her own abuser got away with it; passively she submits to her child's abuse.

The father who was sexually abused as a child, often abuses children himself. According to Steven Wolf, codirector of Northwest Treatment Associates in Seattle, who has been involved in the diagnosis or treatment of four thousand sexual offenders, research data indicate that 50 to 80 percent of adult sexual offenders share histories of abuse in their families of origin. They saw that their own abusers suffered no consequences, and they expect the same good fortune for themselves. Boys who are abused in early childhood may begin as early as seven or eight years old abusing other children. By the time he marries, the abuser has developed a pattern and habit of using children for his own pleasure.

Sexual abuse is habit-forming. "The addiction is as powerful as addiction to heroin," Steven Wolf told me. A person who really wants to stop abusing faces a constant struggle which must be won each day all over again.

Another factor which helps the family keep the secret is society's stress on the supreme authority of the family over children, and the privacy of the family domain.

Several years ago when I was engaged in parish ministry, a

thirteen-year-old girl dropped into my office to see me. She told me of her father's beatings with a heavy leather strap. He also forced her to stand naked in the shower while he stood there and turned on the cold water. This happened repeatedly.

I knew that I was legally obliged to report any case of child abuse, but I hoped to resolve the problem with counseling.

The child ran away from home again and again, always ending up in my office. Finally, she refused to go home.

I explained that I would make a report, a police officer would come and take her to juvenile detention; she would probably be placed in a foster home.

Never had I imagined the hostility and anger that would be directed at me because of my report.

The parents threatened to bring me to court. "Feel free," I said.

They talked to the pastor and to neighbors who belonged to my parish. Nobody understood how I could possibly interfere in a family when that request had not been initiated by the parents.

To my explanation that the child had been abused they responded that she was "difficult," and the father was only disciplining her.

We now know that only a small fraction of cases of sexual abuse of children or adolescents is ever reported. The abuse usually comes to light, if ever, when an adult victim enters therapy for problems in interpersonal relationships; through an anonymous survey; or when some social agency has uncovered the sexual abuse and, in the course of the casework, the mother becomes able to unburden herself.

Why does the adult woman maintain the secrecy?

A woman sexually abused as a child—and this is even more true for men—feels that she is damaged goods, not a whole person, and that anybody to whom she talks will think less of her. Moreover, she carries a burden of guilt. Was the sex her fault? Did she lead on her dad or her uncle or whoever it may have been?

Reinforcing the woman's fear of revealing the secret is the secrecy maintained by social workers and others in the helping professions, and their reluctance to hear about or deal with the issue.

When psychologist Lenore Walker tried to determine the incidence of incest suffered by women who later became battered wives, she devised a series of specific questions for her researchers to present to the women, rather than allow interviewers to ask general questions because, she stated, "We found that interviewers were as likely as our subjects to avoid hearing details, especially in cases of incest." Women who sense that the other person would rather not hear about incest have their own sense of shame and embarrassment heightened thereby.

Doctors R. L. Pierce and Lois H. Pierce, in their analysis of sexual abuse hot-line reports, note that even protective-service workers are often poorly prepared to perform the difficult task of treating the sexually abused child and his or her family. The purpose of the Pierces' analysis was the development of findings which would aid both protective-service workers and therapists in working with such families. If protective-service workers display discomfort in this area, they reinforce the family secret.

That they do so, the Pierces observe, is obvious from the fact that one-third of the cases picked up by the sexual-abuse hot line had already been seen by protective services, without the workers having noted the sexual abuse.

Sexually abused children may mask their real problem by displaying behavior and learning difficulties. Professionals working with such children may prefer treating the symptoms to diagnosing the underlying problem. Their avoidance may well be unconscious, but children who sense that discomfort grow up into adults reluctant to talk about their early abuse.

My conversations with sexually abused children grown to womanhood sometimes reveal that they did attempt to get help with the consequences of their abuse but met therapists unwilling to accept and treat their basic difficulty.

The entire cloak of secrecy—the failure of those designated as "helpers" to see the childhood sexual abuse, the general unspoken apprehension that the secret might get out and explode into terror, the sense that the whole problem is too shameful to talk about—creates an atmosphere which can make it impossible for adult women to talk about their early victimization. And yet, none of the above is done consciously.

Those few women who do dare to speak about the abuse openly, hoping that today's children may be given more adequate attention and protection, are likely to be greeted with consternation. "How *can* you talk about that publicly! What about your husband and children? At least think of them." In other words, the woman's early experience was so shameful that her husband and children will be stained by her open admission. Yet the husband and children had nothing whatever to do with it.

Another danger for the woman who decides to go public is the constant threat of lawsuits. Childhood sexual abuse is very private and secret by its nature. If it was not addressed when it occurred, it can be proved only with great difficulty in later life. Even if addressed in childhood, abuse is difficult to prove, and the nonabusing parent may want to avoid pressing charges for that reason.

A mother who discovered that her husband had sexually abused their children and who divorced him, told me that she is willing to talk publicly about her experience. She said, "Until we who have been through the harassment and the pain speak out, this situation will not change."

I agree.

As a woman, however, I doubt that I myself would have the courage to talk publicly about this kind of pain, had it happened to me. That is why I so admire the many women whose personal courage enabled them to break the silence in the pages of this book.

For the sake of the children.

Until society *wants* to hear, only the brave will accept the challenge to put their anguish into words.

Men sexually abused as children tend not to talk about it at all. Sexual abuse attacks the very fabric of their masculinity.

A good friend of mine spent some years in Alcatraz. Since his release, he has devoted so many years of his life to volunteer work in behalf of teenagers and the relatives of prisoners that he was recently honored by the President. Knowing that prisoners are the population most likely to have suffered childhood sexual abuse, I asked him whether he was aware of childhood sex abuse among his fellow prisoners. "No," he said, "I never heard of it."

He offered to talk with another released prisoner, and question him. "Yes," he reported back, "my friend was sexually abused as a child, but he won't talk to anybody about it."

Even though confined together the men had not discussed their childhood abuse.

A couple of months ago I visited a prisoner in a men's correctional center. I didn't know him, but went along with a friend. "What work do you do?" the prisoner asked me.

"I'm a writer."

"What are you writing now?"

"A book on childhood sexual abuse in the home."

The effect on him was electrifying. He jumped in his chair, clenched his fists, and through gritted teeth said, "Don't talk about that to me. I can't even *think* about it." And he changed the subject.

He had probably been abused as a child. Among his other crimes, he had committed rape. Statistically, men who rape are likely to have been *heterosexually* assaulted in childhood. In fact, California psychologists M. Petrovich and D. Templer from the California School of Professional Psychology in Fresno have found a high rate of such assault among one group: rapists. Three psychologists found that, of eighty-three convicted rapists in a California prison, 59 percent reported having been heterosexually molested before the age of sixteen.

As Steven Wolf pointed out to me, victimization as a child plays an important role in the later development of male sexual abusers.

Psychologist A. N. Groth, director of the Connecticut Sex Offenders Program, in a study of offenders conducted among prisoners and mental health patients, reports that 81 percent were sexually victimized as children.

As children they maintained secrecy for probably the same

reasons as girls: fear, threats, shame, guilt, probable disruption of their families.

But then they began finding their own victims, and had done so by age fourteen, as an average. According to the Juvenile Sexual Offender Program at the University of Washington's Adolescent Clinic, the average age of their victims is six. Two-thirds of the abusing adolescents molest children while babysitting. Children so young, whether boys or girls, won't tell if threatened. As adult men these molesters won't want to tell mental health professionals if they have continued molesting, because they don't want to get caught. (Not all children who are molested become molesters in turn, of course, but a significant percentage do.)

In this regard I did hear one beautiful story.

Helen's children, including her son, had been sexually abused by their father.

Having divorced the husband, she took part in a weekend called a "Beginning Experience," a gentle closing of one phase of her life, in this case her marriage, with forgiveness for whatever wrongs were endured and the initiation of a new beginning. In the course of the weekend she wrote a final letter to her husband. The letter was not written to be mailed, but to reach closure.

Shortly after the weekend, Helen's adult son dropped in to visit her. "I'd like you to hear the closing letter I wrote to your father," she said, and read it aloud. Both of them wept. Then the son said, "Mom, I need to tell you something; I have the same problem as Dad." Quietly, they were able to discuss the son's compulsion to abuse other children.

Few mothers can create such an atmosphere of love and trust with their adult sons; few sons can respond with so much courage and openness. Both of them had won a victory.

Moreover, they demonstrated that a mother and son can share this deeply.

Vicki Wagner, of Seattle's Orion Center, told me that "most street kids have been sexually abused; we didn't catch all of it earlier because we didn't realize how deep a sense of trust boys need to develop before they can talk about it. Our caseworkers are aware of that now."

Lastly, why do *I* think family childhood sexual abuse is kept so secret?

Frankly, had it happened to me, I doubt that I would ever have had the courage to tell.

I'm proud of my father and enjoy talking about him. Because he was a loving, talented and gifted person, I am enhanced by our relationship.

Had he thought so little of himself and me as to have abused me for his selfish pleasure, I would have felt so diminished, so trivialized, that I would have repressed the memory. I could never have told even my mother.

To the extent that I am proud of my father's character, so would I be ashamed of his failure to respect me.

Why some professionals, psychiatrists, counselors, social workers, therapists, should strive for secrecy, I understand all too well.

The shame of incest overwhelms us. We feel soiled in acknowledging its presence. Perhaps we are embarrassed to discover it hidden among the people we work with. Or perhaps we don't want to have to suspect everybody.

Why does society prefer not to know? For those kinds of reasons which kept German citizens ignorant of the extermination camps during World War II. It's too terrible to know about. Besides, if we *do* acknowledge its presence, our consciences would force us to take action. We'd rather not. Action might be dangerous. Passivity is more suited to the tenor of our lives.

If we, as a nation of concerned citizens, admitted the frequency of incest, where would it all end?

We'd be invading the sanctity of the home, a treasured American heritage.

And what would we do with all the offenders? How would we care for the abused children? Who would pay for it all? That's the crunch. We think it better to mind our own business and avoid problems requiring so much money, time, and personnel.

As these stories creep out, and we are forced to recognize the frequency of family sexual abuse, we are overwhelmed. It's like opening Pandora's box. Instinct moves us to jam the lid back on.

Increasing numbers of sexually abused children hit the city streets. We can close our eyes to that phenomenon; street kids have little visibility during the daytime. Or, if we do notice, we can tell ourselves they're incorrigibles who should get a good paddling, and shrug them off.

That doesn't make them go away. Sooner or later, the problem of street kids will burgeon into one of such magnitude that constructive steps will have to be taken. So we think: I don't need to worry about it. I've got enough worries. Leave it for the next generation.

Anyhow, they're not *my* kids, and I've got too much else to do to be my brother's keeper.

FIVE

Marilyn

OF ALL the brave women I have met in the past year, she is certainly one of the most courageous.

Here I call her Marilyn.

Marilyn knew that something was wrong with her children and with her husband, although she could not put her finger on it and nobody was talking. She went to the priest in her parish for help. "Does your husband drink?" he asked. "No, Father."

"Work hard?"

"Yes."

"Gamble?"

"No."

"Run around with other women?"

"No."

"Some women," he said, "really have problems.

"You have a husband who takes a lot of responsibility, works hard, supports his family, and you're 'upset' about something. You ought to be thanking God for your good fortune."

Marilyn left the rectory, walked into the church, and wept nonstop for three hours. Two more years passed before she discovered that her husband had sexually abused every one of her three daughters, and two adopted sons. "If only," she says, "if only the subject had not been kept so secret, if only ministers and priests also knew about it, the tragedy of our family might not have occurred.

"I had not been married more than a year when I realized that something was wrong with our marriage, dreadfully wrong. If only I had known as much about the sexual abuse of children as I have since learned, I could have prevented tragedy. But nobody talked about it then."

When I met Marilyn I was impressed by her air of quiet serenity, the sense of inner strength and stability which she radiated without effort. I guessed her to be in her mid-forties; I knew that her life had been traumatic.

She welcomed me graciously, as did her teenage daughter who wore a lovely dress which, she was proud to tell me, she had made for herself.

The interview was going to be difficult for Marilyn, I knew. Later I could search for the source of strength and stability and the reason for her gracious willingness to talk with me.

I took the plunge. "When did you first find out that your husband was sexually abusing your children? And how many of your children?"

"My three children, the oldest of whom was then fifteen, and two adopted boys." She shuddered. Just a small movement, but I caught it.

"Six years ago I heard my fifteen-year-old daughter scream from one of the sheds. I ran out to her. Joe, my husband, was there, and he was replacing his belt. 'What happened?' I asked.

"My daughter fled. My husband was in no mood for communication; he wouldn't talk.

"When my daughter returned I again asked, 'What's wrong?'

"'Mother,' she said, 'I don't want Dad ever to help me. With anything. I don't need him.'

"'But,' I answered 'your dad needs to help you children more. You're working too hard. Why not?'

"'I don't want him. I just don't want him around. I'm afraid of him.'

"'Why?'

"'Mother,' she sobbed, 'I'm not a virgin, and I haven't been since I was ten years old.'

"Appalled, I began asking questions. And more questions.

"Researched in the community.

"Talked to Joe's family.

"I discovered that Joe's mother had been a sexually-abused child; Joe's father had abused him and his sisters when they were children. It was the family secret, handed down from generation to generation. They were angry at me for breaking the seal.

"My husband had been abusing children in the community long before he ever married me; he had abused his own sisters and cousins. It had become a family legacy."

Marilyn's mother-in-law had never spoken of her childhood sexual abuse to anybody until Marilyn questioned her; talking about it was frightening. Marilyn's father-in-law was glad for the opportunity of talking about his own misdeeds: the abuse he had inflicted on children, mostly relatives. He was elderly, and wanted to get squared away before he died.

Actually, he had gone to a priest once before to talk about his problem. The priest had counselled him to remain with his

family, keep it intact. That had happened in the '40s or early
'50s when child sexual abuse was a big secret and nobody
talked about it, so most people never knew it was going on.

He had stayed with his family, but he couldn't stop the
child abuse. He did struggle, but it had become a compulsion.
He had abused his son, Joe, and he knew that Joe, in his turn,
was abusing neighborhood children. Where would the nightmare end? He didn't know, and he didn't know where to get
help.

The priest to whom he had once gone asking for assistance
had married Joe and Marilyn. He had given Marilyn no warn-
ing. Probably those errors were not the priest's fault; nobody
knew the crippling effects of child sexual abuse, because it
was kept closely guarded: the family's deepest secret.

In fact, Joe had been abusing the neighbor's children while
he was courting Marilyn; those children had never talked
about the abuse either. Now that concerned parents began
asking direct questions, they found some children relieved
because they were given the opportunity of talking about the
abuse they had suffered.

Not one of Marilyn's children had known that their father
was abusing another sister or brother. As Joe selected his
children he told each that if he or she ever told, he would personally kill the child and kill Marilyn as well. The threat was
effective.

The very day that the fifteen-year-old "told," Marilyn confronted her husband.

"Weren't you afraid?" I asked.

"I was too angry to be afraid."

That night Marilyn went to bed, laid her head on a feather
pillow which felt like a block of steel, and prayed: "God, I've
come to you for all kinds of things, and I always knew what to

ask for. Right now, I don't even know what to ask.

"I've got a lot of matters to resolve in the morning, so please give me a good sleep. I have no idea how to proceed, or where to go. Help me."

In the morning, Marilyn started the car, put her hands on the steering wheel, and asked God to point the way. She drove to Mass and talked to the assistant pastor. He referred her to a counselor and to Children's Protective Services. She phoned the latter. A caseworker drove to the home, and again Marilyn confronted Joe, this time with the caseworker. Joe left the house, Marilyn started proceedings for a divorce.

Marilyn sighed. "Once you involve the legal system, it takes over." Taking over meant that the children were each interviewed by fifteen different people, most of them men. "None of my children would get into counseling. They could not, they said, *absolutely could not* tell that story one more time."

Joe was sentenced to seventy days in the sex offenders' program at a psychiatric hospital. Because he proved totally uncooperative, he was returned to court. The judge gave him three to ten years. With good behavior, he got out in three. He had ruined the lives of countless numbers of children. Nobody knows how many children; nobody knows how many more have not yet told; nobody knows how many are his victims now.

Joe promised the judge that he would leave the state and never return. But he had also promised Marilyn and the children that they would get theirs, he would see to that. "Aren't you afraid?"

"Yes."

Marilyn cannot let the fear paralyze her, she knows. After the divorce, with all the bills paid, Marilyn had $4,000,

no job, and no home. She has a small home now, a home ir-
radiated, somehow, with her own inner peace. "I trust God to
take care of us," she says simply.

The children appear to be getting along well: no drugs or
alcohol, no prostitution. But they are experiencing problems
with interpersonal relationships.

"I have problems, too," says Marilyn. "I'm looking at men
again, and occasionally dating. But I take a very hard look at
the men.

"I share my problems with my children, so they know that
I'm struggling, too, and trying to grow. Hearing of my pain,
they may be able to confront their own.

"This entire situation was very difficult for my parents, and
for my younger sister. We've spent a lot of time talking about
it. My brothers don't say much, but they are quietly supportive."

"And from where," I asked, "do you get your own inner
calm?"

"In '79 it seemed as though I was in court, in one way or
another, every week for months. I had five children to support at home. I found one part-time job, and then found a second, and took both. I closed down our family business, dis-
persed the assets, and got prepared for a legal divorce. The
thought that I had to begin all over again drained me. I felt
terrible.

"Then I found a wonderful group of people at a retreat on
healing. I had no idea what might happen. What did happen
was incredible.

"I met loving, caring, prayerful people. They belonged to
different religious denominations. They cared about God, and
they cared about *me*.

"Not only did I experience an inner healing, I realized that

God has a mission for me, a particular mission because of my own specific pain.

"I've belonged to that healing ministry ever since.

"I don't hesitate to speak of my own burden. Again and again, as I do, somebody says, 'That happened to me when I was a child, and I have never talked to anybody.' I encourage them, and pray for their inner healing too."

It was eight years ago that she went to her parish priest to discuss a possible divorce. The sense that something was terribly wrong was pervasive, but she could not understand what it was.

The priest called Joe in, and asked whether he had any problems. "None," said Joe. "Any problems in this marriage are Marilyn's."

That's when the priest asked Marilyn if her husband drank, if he worked, if he beat the children, if he ran around with other women, if he gambled.

There are women in this world, said the priest, who have real problems. You are sitting here complaining about a man who is tired, takes a lot of responsibility, works hard, and is doing his best.

"Yes, Father." Marilyn left. The women always get blamed.

"If only," Marilyn repeats, "it had earlier been acceptable to talk about child sexual abuse in public, if only I could have known about it or talked to somebody else who did, I could have figured out what was wrong with our marriage. I could have remedied the situation long before, fitted the pieces into the puzzle.

"Thank God, we can talk about it now.

"That my story may relieve some other person's pain is my prayer."

SIX

"I Feel Old"

THE legacy of childhood sexual abuse within the family stays with an individual for a lifetime, often manifesting itself in serious long-term problems of adjustment and behavior.

First, there are the immediate effects of the abuse and enforced secrecy on children.

Frequently, the child develops school problems, or drops out of school. Every elementary and junior high school in the country today has several students currently being sexually abused within their families and several more aching from the trauma of past sexual abuse. As soon as the child feels able to venture out on her own, she or he may run away, abruptly terminating education. One youngster I know ran away from home and incest at age eleven and has foraged for herself on the streets ever since. Today she is eighteen. "I feel old," she told me, "I feel like I've lived for a long, long time."

Physical pain usually accompanies forced relations in young children. One girl with whom sex was initiated at eight suffered from a ruptured cervix; another with whom it was started at six told me that the experience was very painful.

Only a few weeks ago a social worker told me of an eighteen-month-old baby who was taken from the family by Children's Protective Services and placed in a foster home. The family was allowed visiting privileges, and they took the baby home overnight. When she was returned, the foster mother noticed what looked like burns on the baby's thighs. She brought the child to a doctor.

According to the physician, the baby's legs had been tied apart and she had been raped. What the ensuing trauma will be for so young a child can only be surmised.

With the spread of sexually transmitted diseases, children are increasingly becoming infected while they are being exploited. Most children's hospitals now have wards for the treatment of sexually transmitted diseases.

No good studies have been made of the long-term psychological, behavioral, and physical effects of early childhood sexual abuse in the home. My own experience convinces me that childhood sexual abuse in the home has profound implications for the whole child welfare system. At least some of these children need intensive individual and group therapy. Unless they are provided with that long-term help which they need, they may suffer serious personality damage throughout life.

Suicide might be one of the effects. Dr. Judith Herman, of Harvard Medical School, in the course of her study of forty female incest victims, found that 38 percent had tried to kill themselves.

The betrayal of a child by someone he or she has learned to trust and depend on almost inevitably leads to such serious emotional problems as poor self-image, guilt, anxiety, suppressed rage, fear of intimacy, sexual promiscuity, and serial marriages.

A recent study conducted at the New York State Psychiatric Institute with adult victims of childhood incest revealed additional characteristics: lack of assertiveness, fear that their own children will be abused, shame, helplessness, and sleep disturbances.

Psychotherapy may help adults who were sexually molested as children, and who display a range of problem behaviors. Therapy may be a slow process but, in my experience, most adults who get it have eventually been able to resolve their conflicts.

Some long-term effects of childhood sexual abuse which I have seen in teenagers with whom I have worked, and women in Good Shepherd treatment centers around the U.S., and which I have noted in the recent professional literature, are:

—Suicide attempts;
—Extended personality problems such as guilt, fear, depression, and anxiety;
—Psychiatric problems, self-mutilation, and a chronically destructive lifestyle;
—Excessive drug and alcohol use;
—Severe problems in interpersonal relationships;
—Fear of marital sexual relations.

Given a check for Christmas by a woman who requested that it go to the poorest of poor children, I dropped by Seattle's Orion Center with the request that it go to a needy street kid.

Director Vicki Wagner told me about one adolescent boy who had run away from home because of family sexual abuse, and then discovered that he could support himself on the streets only by selling sex. In despair he tried to kill himself. He was found in time and put in a hospital. On release, however, he had no place to go. I was glad to leave the check for him, and only wished that I had much more money to give.

The suicide attempt had failed. Undoubtedly, he will make many more; one of them may be successful.

Sometimes children who run away from home because of sexual abuse are severely punished for the running.

One Good Shepherd Sister told me of a thirteen-year-old girl with whom she had worked for several years, who had run away from home at that early age because her stepmother was sexually torturing the child. She and another girl hid in some woods; for food and clothing, they stole from the homes of nearby farmers.

The girls were apprehended. Because the thirteen-year-old girl had both run away from home and stolen food, she was put in solitary confinement in juvenile detention for three months, her food shoved in and out through a hole at the bottom of the door. That the teenager was able even to survive this treatment is testimony to her inner strengths.

As principal of Good Shepherd schools, I have worked with a number of teens who were sexually assaulted at home. Because of their inability to trust, coupled with their depression and fear, to describe those youngsters as "difficult" can be an understatement. Without help their personality problems can catapult them into one misadventure after the other.

Some Good Shepherd Sisters work in psychiatric facilities, in their own practice as family therapists, or they may have specialized treatment programs within their own residential centers.

One six-year-old child stayed with her grandmother while her mother worked. She complained that she was tired of having her male cousin put his finger on her. In therapy she cried and cried, but with anatomically correct dolls showed what she meant. "She needed psychotherapy for a year," said Sister.

Another six-year-old, a boy, was referred for treatment because he appeared nervous, confused, and performed poorly in school. He couldn't learn; his teachers were frustrated. According to a psychologist, he suffered from more than a learning block. Using play therapy with dolls, the clinician discovered that the boy was being sexually abused by several members of his extended family. With extensive psychotherapy, this child recovered from the trauma.

One fourteen-year-old boy who was hospitalized could not talk about sex at all. Mention the word and he froze, immobilized. He would chat casually with other adolescents, but could not discuss his problem. Whether therapists were ever able to reach him I don't know.

An eleven-year-old girl had dropped out of school and refused to return, staying in the house most of the day. She just sat, doing nothing; occasionally she turned on the TV. When questioned she did not respond to her caseworker. She was accepted in a Good Shepherd Home where, gradually, her appearance and manner improved. Then she began enjoying school. It turned out that her father had sexually assaulted her, and she had supposed she must be pregnant as a result. With that fear relieved she could again pick up the pieces of her life. But she needed intensive counseling over a long period.

I have myself worked with adolescents placed in Good Shepherd Homes because of promiscuous behavior. Occasionally—and I really don't know how often, because teenagers, like children, seldom talk about sex abuse—the story of incest would come out. The mother might have divorced the abusing father, but she had not taken the children to a therapist as she had been advised. She had thought that therapy was unnecessary until the promiscuous behavior developed. Then she wanted help for the adolescents and help for herself in controlling them, but it may have come too late. Some children are so damaged that therapy can take a long time.

Adolescents suffer greatly when mothers deny the incest and blame the daughters. One teenager in a Good Shepherd Home expressed anger and defiance. Her parents threatened never to see her again unless she retracted her lies about her father's abuse. The girl would not do that. She missed seeing her brothers and sisters, whom she really loved. Her grandparents did come to see her, and that helped. When the time came for her to leave, the grandparents said they would be willing to take her into their home, but she would have to retract her accusations. Because the girl did not want to go to a foster home, she retracted them. The child bore a heavy burden. Her parents were legally prohibited from seeing her at her grandparents' home, and in the end, she did adjust successfully to life.

I recall a seriously emotionally disturbed girl sent by the court to a Home in which I was the principal. According to the allegations of her father, she had lied about him. Her father was cleared in court, and Maryanne was sent to us.

She had accused her father of forcing her to have oral sex with him. To those who knew the father, that seemed incredible. He was known as a good stalwart member of his church and community, and his lawyer had defended him well.

Because Maryanne was so emotional, it was not difficult to believe that she had fantasized the whole episode, not at all hard for an experienced attorney to get her to contradict herself in court.

I had engaged a registered nurse to teach health and hygiene. She came to me one day, very distressed. "Maryanne can't be lying," she said. "She has talked to me at length. She describes details which she could not have known without the experience."

Maryanne wasn't lying. Of course she wasn't lying. But she was so emotionally disturbed by the trauma which she had already endured that a defense attorney could manipulate her into saying almost anything. Then, too, her behavior had become so negative, so unbalanced, that people could easily assume that she had lied about her father—a "good" man— simply because, as he said, he had tried to stop her from running around with every Johnny-on-the-block.

Perhaps we cannot blame ourselves for refusing to see what we would prefer not to be so.

I have come to know, and tried to help, a young woman who has had serious psychotic breaks because of the incest perpetrated by her father. Her psychiatrist doubts that she can ever totally recover; she cannot accept work other than housekeeping because the slightest degree of responsibility shatters her. Outwardly warm and loving, she lives in a shell so fragile that I have hesitated even to tap it. From the day she met me she wanted to share her story and did so freely.

Encouraged by that, and surprised, I tried to forge a relationship, but found her so insecure that I have never ventured beyond the threshold.

Sexually abused children may tend to be self-mutilating because they blame themselves for the "seduction" of their fathers. Often, they have also been blamed by others.

In Good Shepherd Homes in which I have worked I have seen bright, beautiful, talented teenage girls inserting beads under their fingernails, or under the first layer of skin on their hands, or cutting themselves without intending suicide. Until they can bring themselves to talk about the sexual molestation, they seem unable to relieve themselves of the depression and guilt.

Sometimes that takes years.

Adult women who were sexually abused in childhood sometimes tend to select a self-punishing lifestyle. Because of their sense of guilt in allowing the incest (although, actually, they had no choice), they may make those life choices which lay them open to physical abuse. Battered women, in particular, often typify this way of life.

A therapist and consultant to the New York State Department of Social Services, Dr. John Migenes, points out that a woman who has been sexually abused may be attracted to the pseudo-macho male: powerful, as she had perceived her father to be. She thinks that the man can take care of her and make her decisions, but he usually abuses this power and relegates her to the victim role for which her relationship with her father had prepared her. The marriage, or the succession of marriages, are not likely to be happy. Unfortunately this woman's sons, without intervention, may become abusers in their turn. The cycle endlessly repeats itself.

Psychologist Lenore Walker, in her study of the battered-woman syndrome, states that almost one-half of her sample of battered women reported that they were the victims of sexual assault in childhood. Study of the data revealed that the sexual assault was a repeated occurrence. Male relatives were reported as the most frequent perpetrators.

Walker's findings agree with the experience of after-care workers and Sisters I have talked to who work in shelters for battered women operated by the Good Shepherd Sisters all over the country.

Over 50 percent, probably more, they report, had been sexually abused in their own homes as children.

The Sisters do not ask personal questions; the information given them is volunteered. Some battered women were abused by every male who visited their homes: fathers, brothers, cousins, mother's boy friends. As a result, their self-esteem could be measured only in negatives; these women may be impulsive, reaching out for whatever satisfaction they can get, here and now; and they may fear to trust anybody.

Some battered women who flee to the shelters do divorce their husbands. But without intensive guidance they may simply marry another batterer. The motivating factor, all too unconscious, is the learned helplessness.

These women may have never experienced a childhood. They may play games with their children by the hour and enjoy them on the children's level because they are living on that level themselves. They never had a chance to enjoy the usual pastimes of children and adolescents.

Fear and guilt, carried to extremes, may make some battered women feel incapable of raising sons. These women may give their sons up for adoption, not because they don't love them, but because they cannot handle one more male person in their lives.

Rosa, for example, is making it, but only just. She wanted an apartment close to the shelter so that she could find support from the Sisters there, but both the first and second apartments that she tried were too small. Then she moved into the same complex as her mother.

During Rosa's childhood, spent with her mother, she was sexually abused by a variety of relatives. Just living in that same area recalls a lot she would like to forget.

Rosa is impulsive. Because she has had so few satisfactions during life, she feels that she must grab for whatever she can get, right now. She finds it very difficult to trust anybody.

Rosa did leave her abuser-husband. But she has had difficulty accepting her son, and seldom, if ever, touches or hugs him. It's fine with Rosa for the Sisters and after-care worker to put arms around the child and hold him tight, because she knows that he needs that from some woman. The after-care worker, Pearl, understands that attitude, because that's the way Pearl once felt about her own son.

Lilian had lived in an abusive situation with her husband for three years before deciding to leave him. He had had brain surgery and had been committed to a psychiatric hospital for a year. Then Lilian had supported him for three more years. But he flew into rages, almost killed her a couple of times, and flung the children, including the baby, across the room.

Lilian was not assertive. She invited people to walk all over her. Her own mother had been an alcoholic. When her children were young, she had stuffed their mouths full of rags so they couldn't cry out, and then gone out on the town. Lilian's mother would also bleed money out of her. The young woman did get a factory job and shared a car with her mother. They had a fight, so the mother took the car to prevent Lilian from getting to work.

With that background, Lilian could not possibly be assertive; she allowed herself to be used. Everybody used her. And her husband used her most of all.

Lilian, of course, had been sexually abused as a child. By whom? By everybody: her father, brother, uncle, mother's boyfriends. Lilian had been raised to be a victim.

Married at fifteen, she already had three children.

"She stayed at the shelter five months," says Sister Susan. "We tried to teach her to meet her own needs first. We stressed her own importance as a person. We explained that if she never took time for herself, she'd be cranky with her youngsters.

"A good worker, she's still in the factory. She makes enough money for rent and food, but not enough for a babysitter. We paid the first month's rent and the security deposit, and were able to scrounge furniture for her. Lilian phones back at least every three weeks and just talks . . . about herself, her children, her feelings. She needs friends, and we're glad to be those friends."

Drug and alcohol addiction are avenues of pain which also may be selected by the child sexually abused at home.

Good Shepherd Sisters operate drug and alcohol rehabilitation centers in this country. Sometimes they work with alcoholics from alcohol treatment centers established by other agencies. I have myself worked with both juveniles and adults addicted to alcohol and/or drugs.

Good Shepherd Sister Maureen Crayne, a social worker who has counseled in places from St. Paul to Kaneohi, Hawaii, reflected on the alcoholic women to whom she has offered love and friendship as they struggled to free themselves of their addiction.

Sister Maureen remembers Bridget, a middle-aged woman and an Irish Catholic. Having been sexually abused by her father, Bridget had a variety of problems with sexual relations in marriage. The marriage broke up, and she began wondering if she might be a lesbian. Grappling with this problem from her own particular religious viewpoint, Bridget began drinking to drown some of her sorrows, and then she advanced into serious alcoholism.

Her efforts to recover were blocked by her guilt: if she was a lesbian—and she did not really know—then God could not forgive her.

In any case, she could not and never would be able to forgive her father. Not that Bridget did not try. She struggled to make herself forgive, she wrestled with forgiveness. But she simply could not forgive.

"I can't say the Lord's Prayer," she once said sorrowfully in a group therapy session. "I can't ask God to forgive my sins as I forgive others, because I don't forgive. If I pray the Our Father, I am really asking God not to forgive me."

Sister Maureen explained to Bridget that God does not ask us to feel forgiveness for a person who has seriously wronged us if we can't feel it. God asks us only to try. God knows what we can't do, and he accepts the willingness to forgive if we could.

"Some day," Bridget's counselor added, "you will feel able to forgive your father. Wait for that time to come, and don't worry about it in the meantime.

"God is bigger than our constraints and our fears; we can't limit God. Let's hope *we* can forgive some day, and that's enough."

After that session, Sister Maureen hugged Bridget. "Because she's a Catholic, that hug from a Sister signified God's love for her, as well as mine," said Sister. "Often that hug is more healing than any of my words."

Many alcoholic women have been sexually abused as children, says Sister Maureen. Even as youngsters they learned that going to bed with a brother-in-law or a brother or some relative was rewarded by a supply of alcohol. Their craving for alcohol overcame their moral values. Although they hated themselves for it, to get the alcohol they needed, they willingly went to bed with whatever relative provided them with drinks. "That," Sister said, "is a fairly frequent way for sexual abuse to lead into addiction, and for addiction then to promote sexual abuse."

One woman, sexually abused by her father, at fifteen met a man who offered her percodan and methaline in return for her sexual favors. The drugs offered her the escape she craved and she became addicted quickly. After their marriage, he kept her adequately supplied and got her totally hooked. Then he took her to a city especially noted for its casinos, set her up in a hotel, and sent in his friends. "He got me into orgies," she said. "He was supposed to protect me, but he used me. I hated it, but I needed the drugs. After five years I got the courage to phone my mother and get on the plane for home.

My mother purposely sent me no money, only a plane ticket, so I couldn't buy drinks on the plane. Even the stewardess on the plane had been asked not to serve me drinks. But I made friends with the man in the seat ahead of me, and he bought me the drinks I craved.

"By the time I got to my home town, I had been knocked out for a week. My new 'friend' and I had spent that week together in a hotel. I hated myself and I hated the alcohol and pills, but my body craved them, and I couldn't help it.

"I got so disgusted with myself that I had to drink to drown the disgust and despair.

"Victimized by sexual abuse as a child, I went on to become victimized again by drugs and alcohol. Now it's killing me. I *have* to get off."

Says Sister Maureen, "Alcoholic women need to develop a new lifestyle, a new beginning, and to let grievances go. Those who suffered through family sexual assault need to come to terms with their sexuality and with their previous victimization by men. They need help to see themselves as persons and as women who ought to be respected.

"Male dependence goes along with drug dependence. Alcoholic women may have a man or two or more in the background whom they can manipulate into giving them alcohol and money; they call these men their 'stashes.' They can be married to one man, but have a couple of stashes as safeties against the day they might not have money for a drink. Giving up those stashes is critical in the struggle against alcohol.

"One stash I heard of did not ask the woman for sex at all, but the money he provided enabled her to remain an alcoholic. Perhaps what he got out of it was a sense of moral superiority. Regardless, a woman who wants sobriety has to surrender the male dependence before she can totally give up the alcoholic dependence.

"I recall one woman alcoholic who told me quietly, 'I turned my life over to God last night.' I took that with a grain of salt. But I watched her peacefully surrender that old life, bit by bit, and it was a tough life to hand over to God.

"Sexually abused by her father, she had been gang-raped when she was a teenager. She had stood by and watched people killed. Although she was not directly involved herself, the killers were her friends. Like many sexually abused women, she felt that she ought to 'save' her father.

"Day after day after day she struggled to let one need go after the other. I realized that her spiritual surrender had indeed been very real. She meant it.

"The struggle isn't over, of course; it will never be over. Sobriety is a battle an alcoholic has to win all over again, every day. Actually, it's a life-and-death struggle. Not everybody makes it. It calls for rigorous honesty and a willingness to let go of every obstructing dependence.

"I admire those women. And I think to myself that if I were that single-hearted and generous in my pursuit of God, I would have achieved sanctity long before now."

I was on the staff of St. Patrick's Parish, Seattle, when my pastor and a Lutheran minister, Reverend Nyer Urness, decided to establish a night shelter for street men. Because I had developed our social-justice and outreach programs, I got involved with the shelter. We started it almost six years ago and established, also, a transition home for men transferring from the street life to the straight life, or resolving other problems.

Immanuel Lutheran Church provided the facilities in both cases. I pledged to provide the money needed for the first couple of years, and several thousand dollars a year after that.

Three years ago I gave one evening a week to purchase and prepare food for that night's hot dinner. We provided dinner to as many as ninety men at night, and shelter for up to fifty men (although we kept telling ourselves that we couldn't hold more than thirty). On my nights, one of the men, who had been a chef but was currently without a job, took over the cooking. Other men served the food, so I was left to socialize and chat with the men.

I was the only woman present on those nights, and the men gradually became accustomed to me; some of them shared their own lives and difficulties with me. The majority of the men were simply unskilled laborers who couldn't find work.

Bill was middle-aged, usually clean and neat, but seemed to be chronically depressed. He may have been an alcoholic, but men under the influence couldn't stay at our shelter; that would have kept him from drinking for some hours before he headed for the shelter (and I really don't know for sure that he drank at all).

He confided that his childhood had been miserable. His father had been killed in a work-related accident, and he had lived with an uncle who had sexually abused him. He joined the army as soon as he could persuade the recruiters that he was old enough; he completed high school in the army. Having put in nineteen years in the service, he began considering retirement with a good pension.

Stationed in Korea, he met a Korean woman who returned his love. They married and had a little girl. For the first time in his life, Bill enjoyed happiness, and he luxuriated in the feeling. The child was just three when both she and her mother were killed in a train accident. Bill was devastated. Quitting the army, he returned to the States. He was not able to bear living in the country where his loved ones were killed. "They were the only people who ever loved me," said Bill.

He left the army before he qualified for a pension. He had no motivation to pick up steady work, and he did only those menial jobs which earned enough money for him to live on. He would gladly, I could see, have died with his wife and child. Their deaths had ended his life.

Because of his unhappy childhood and youth, and his sense that nobody other than his wife and child had ever loved him, I would guess that Bill will not recover from his grief.

Pastor Urness spent hours of his time counseling the men who came into our lives. People from various churches throughout the city took turns cooking and serving food to the men each night, listening to their stories, demonstrating their belief in the men as worthwhile persons, and showing that they cared. The men tended to share their most intimate stories only with Pastor Urness, although I became privy to some of them during that winter when I was the only woman present.

Men who were sexually abused as children tend, more than women, to turn their sense of rage and helplessness outward into aggressive and antisocial behavior. "Unless they have a very pressing reason," Pastor Urness told me, "men seldom admit that they have been sexually abused as children. I may see every indication that such has happened in their youth, but they talk about it only after they have developed a very deep trust.

"Part of the reason for the men's silence may be due to the

fact that they come to our shelter wrestling with their sexuality, feeling less than men because they are on the streets or have problems with alcohol." (Not all street men, nor even most, have problems with alcohol; many can't find work simply because the jobs they can do are not available.)

"Relatively few men have talked to me about sexual abuse in childhood, and then they talk about the offender as an uncle or cousin or older brother. Never their fathers.

"Men who were sexually abused at home do need to talk about the experience and get counseling, but I'm not sure that any of us know how to make that possible for them."

Without taking a look at the offenders, I would leave this chapter on suffering incomplete. They also endure pain, perhaps more than we know.

One minister told of a man who had asked for counseling. Suddenly, he slid off his chair and onto his knees, begging the minister, with tears streaming down his face, to castrate him right then and there; he had sexually abused his own daughter and doubted that he could control his impulses in the future.

Sister Anna who has worked with sex offenders in a psychiatric setting says, "The offenders are tormented by their knowledge that their sex offenses could happen again."

According to Steven Wolf, "Incest offenders do experience guilt, but never enough to prevent the next offense when the opportunity presents itself."

In a talk given in Lisbon at the Third International Conference on Victimology in November, 1984, Wolf described the offenders as individuals who typically act out impulses in the areas of alcohol, drug abuse, sexual promiscuity, or physical aggression. Their social adjustments are poor. Such men tend to be rebellious, unable to anticipate the consequences of their behavior, incapable of sustaining personal relationships. They blame others for their problems. For instance, according to Wolf, an incestuous father may say, in all seriousness, "But my four-year-old daughter seduced me." They seem to use sexuality in a self-medicating manner, much as the alcoholic abuses that drug. Under stress, they use sexuality to gratify themselves and to avoid dealing with the problem.

These men can look very sociable. They come from every walk in life, and they present a normal appearance. One wonders how such a nice clean-cut fellow could do such horrible things. In treatment, that side of his character may never show, but let something come up that pulls off the veneer, and we see the beast. Roland Summit in California talks about this as *the* conflict between good and evil, and I don't think that idea is far-fetched. For these men, deviant sexuality is as powerful an addiction as heroin. They will rearrange their total lives to incorporate their deviance, sacrifice anybody and anyone.

One might look at these offenders as great white sharks, and their victims as fish in their ocean.

I remember one minister of a small rural fundamentalist church who had been sexually abusing foster children over a number of years. "How can you, a minister of the Lord, do these things?" I asked.

"Because I know the Lord will forgive me," he answered. So he went into every act of sexual abuse telling himself, "The Lord will forgive me; the Lord will let me go."

And I see offenders of every religion: Lutheran, Episcopalian, Catholic, Baptist, Mormon, Jew, Buddhist, atheist—all religions, all walks of life.

A study done at a New York psychiatric facility indicates that sex offenders typically offend all the way across the board: in a case where the initial diagnosis is of incest with a female child, 44 percent also molest children outside of the home; 11 percent also molest their own sons; 18 percent are overt rapists; 18 percent are flashers, and on and on. At Northwest Treatment Associates we never see a man who has offended against only one victim. Statistically, if they have one victim, they have five.

Incest offenders have assaulted victims long before they begin their own families, says Wolf. He recently surveyed a group of sex offenders: 75 percent of the men had begun their sexual adventures in adolescence, initiating their first experience at age eight or nine.

"We see many men who were sexually abused in *their* youth. They passed it on."

Introduced to me, Teresita extended her hand, but it was slightly off course. She seemed to be looking at me, but her eyes were not quite focused where I might have expected. Taking her hand, I noticed a tremor.

As Teresita walked along with me I thought to myself that either she was on drugs right now or she suffered from some neurological impairment, perhaps epilepsy. The young woman was clear-eyed and perceptive as she chatted. Deliberately, I fell behind to notice her walk. That was a bit off, too.

The women at this treatment center had been told that I am a writer and interested in interviewing any person willing to share her life and problems. With a smile, Teresita told me that she was willing to talk.

"Do you have epilepsy?" I asked. "Forgive me, but I can

see that something about your movements is not quite right."

She smiled. "Not epilepsy, a slight touch of cerebral palsy."

"And when did you discover this?"

"In the past year. One of the Sisters took me to a neurologist. She suspected neurological impairment for a condition for which I had been prescribed drugs years ago. I had only walked into the room when the neurologist said, 'You have a mild case of cerebral palsy; hasn't anybody ever told you so?' I'd seen plenty of doctors, but nobody had ever diagnosed it."

"What kind of doctors?"

"Well, a psychiatrist for one. My hand shakes," and she extended both hands, "so he gave me pills to control the trembling. Actually, of course, no pills ever could control this because it's caused by the slight cerebral palsy. Because they didn't work, he kept giving me stronger ones. I became a legal drug addict.

"The pills were free, and they came in the mail. No questions asked. Neither my family nor I could pay for adequate treatment, so I was on a state program, and both the psychiatrist and the pills were free."

"The psychiatrist never suspected cerebral palsy?"

"If so, he never said anything."

"Did he ever suggest a consultation with a neurologist?"

"No."

"Why did you go to a psychiatrist?"

"In junior high school I would sit staring off into space. I got so attached to the school psychologist that I just followed her around, so I was referred for psychiatric help."

"Had you been sexually abused at home?"

"Yes. My stepfather. He was an alcoholic."

"Did the psychiatrist know that?"

"He never asked."

"My own father is a caring person," she said, "but the kind who thinks you can pull yourself up by your bootstraps. He didn't see my need for therapy, never has understood. As for my mother, she's become a legal drug addict too."

"So what did you do with the free pills that came in the mail?"

"My parents got divorced, and then my stepfather . . . well, you know.

"He was an alcoholic, too. So by the time I was a freshman in high school I had begun mixing the pills with alcohol. I was thirteen years old.

"I tried suicide with the drugs many times, at least eleven. The pills were just mailed; nobody checked how I used them. I saved them and took big doses, but somebody always found me in time.

"I made my first suicide attempt when I was in the sixth grade. I got so low, so depressed. I still get depressed, but somebody is always around here for me to talk to.

"I've been here eighteen months and I'm moving out soon. I have loved it here; I love the Sisters.

"After sexual abuse, I just couldn't make it by myself."

Teresita took me into her room and proudly displayed her college diploma, an undergraduate degree in social work. She had completed her education after coming to the Sisters. "Right now is not the time for me to do social work," she said. "I have to take care of myself first. In ten days I'll have been totally off drugs and alcohol for one year. I'm proud of that."

Devastated by incest, some children turn their anger outward and become socially deviant; others may turn the anger inward, endeavoring to destroy themselves by such means as suicide or alcohol or drugs. Young as she is, in her early twenties, Teresita had already tried all three.

The young woman is bright, eager, and good-looking. As I was preparing to leave she said, "People look at me and say, 'You're so young and naive.' But I've already been through more than they'll ever face in a lifetime.

SEVEN

Angela

I WAS born in a small town in a rural area.

When I was two my mother deserted the family. That was thirty years ago. I was two years old. My mother was eighteen.

I was born to be wild. That's why I'm alive to tell my story.

Had I not been born to fight, to fight tough, I'd be a basket case right now, in the back ward of some state hospital.

At age two I knew my mom and dad were having marital problems. I remember them fighting. Dad was beating Mom up and accusing her of running around. Then I was put in with the Oblate Sisters.

Nobody explained why. I couldn't understand. At age three I ran away from there, packed a little suitcase, took it down a long avenue, put it on the pavement and sat on it, thinking, "What do I do now?" Some friends of the Sisters saw me and brought me back. Then they told me that my mother had left me. My dad couldn't take care of me and work too. That's why he had to put me someplace.

I was a behavior problem, "obnoxious," they called it. But I was only trying to get attention, to get into the center of things, because I felt so left out. I needed a mother's love and I wasn't getting it. That made me angry, so I fought.

I loved the other children and the nuns, but I didn't act like it. I wanted attention. If I couldn't get it by being good, I'd be bad.

My mother was only sixteen when I was born. She was too young for marriage, and for all of us kids who came too quickly.

I was a few months over three when I went back home. My parents were living together again. They brought back my older brother, and my retarded brother, Richard, too.

When I was five I started a fire, not intentionally. The house was cold, we kids were shivering. So I went to the basement and stuffed carpet into an old coal furnace. The flames leaped out and caught the diapers hanging on the line to dry. Mom ran next door to use the phone.

My brother Timmy was just born. I got him out and my oldest brother got himself out. But Richard was tied to the bed. He couldn't get out, and I couldn't untie the knots. Mom was standing in the middle of the street, screaming. I crawled under Richard's bed. If he was going to die, so was I. Then my mom rushed in and cut the knots with a butcher knife and we all got out.

The house was demolished. So was I, knowing my mom would have left Richard there to be burned to death. Having a mentally retarded child was a disgrace to my parents.

I started kindergarten and got kicked out. I had horrible problems in school, just terrible, and they didn't get any better. I was so angry, and didn't know what to do.

My parents got divorced and my grandmother, my mother's mother, moved in. She had tremendous anger and beat all of us. We children took turns getting beatings for each other because one person physically could not stand it. Two times out of three, it was me. But if Richard was in the way, he got it.

I was close to six when I walked two and a half miles across town one time to my father because my grandmother had taken a slat from the bed and beaten me black and blue all over. My dad took me to the police station. That station should have the record.

Grandmother made us eat every solitary morsel on our plates, crammed it down our throats. I'm an adult now, but I still have all kinds of problems with food. The dogs were treated better than us kids. In fact, one time she made Timmy eat dog food. All we got to eat, often, was bread and water.

I was always running away from home to Dad's. At age nine I went to him, and he sent me to live for a while with his mother in a distant state.

When I returned, I lived with Dad again. He began taking me around to his friends and acquaintances to show me off. Suddenly I realized that he was not showing off a cute little daughter, he was introducing a mature woman companion. I had to grow up fast. Dad and I went off on a vacation, my first ever, but I was more my dad's girlfriend on that vacation than a daughter to whom he was showing a good time.

I was trying to get through school, but, what with one thing and another, my sexuality awakened. Because of the relationship with Dad, I had become seductive, flirty, and sexually aggressive. My dad fondled me a lot. We didn't have intercourse, but that's about all we didn't do.

I loved my dad as Dad. I began thinking that something must be wrong with him. Then he was accused of rape by one of my school friends. I had to testify before the grand jury.

She was my friend and threatening me. I didn't know for sure, but I figured my dad had probably done it. But my dad was all I had.

I could not go back to my mother; my grandmother didn't want me. Only one person in the whole world loved me: Dad.

Dad tutored me as to what to say to the grand jury. We went over and over it. I lied to the grand jury. I despised myself. But Dad was the only person I had.

From then on he stopped fondling me. I went to school in the same neighborhood. To live with all this was hard. I tried to build up a relationship with God. I got up early so I could go to Mass and Communion every day. I watched the nuns in their habits and veils and knew there had to be Someone for them to live like that.

I didn't dress right, didn't know how. Besides, Dad was now trying to get Richard into a Catholic school and we had to save every bit of money. To get clothing I needed, I shoplifted.

Dad was very stingy, and I didn't get enough to eat. My mother had taught me how to shoplift. It was a racket, really. She'd bring me into a store, show me what to steal, and tell me where to put it. Then she'd wander off by herself, and maybe distract the clerk and I'd steal. Stuff she wanted, like really good underwear and food. My mother loved fancy underwear. To this day, she still collects it.

It went fine until one day I got caught. My mother stood there in the middle of the big store and yelled at me for stealing. I couldn't believe my ears. She had told me to do it, and it was a big-size bra. I wasn't prosecuted, because everybody knows that an eight-year-old child doesn't steal big bras for herself. Well, anyway, I kept stealing food.

I still have a problem with close relationships. As a child, I never formed them, never knew real family. That I am defective in that area, I know. I try to watch it. Nobody knows how hard it is to learn as an adult what could instinctively have been learned as a baby and a small child.

Looking back now, I can understand much more. My mother was left with four children to support. She was very young for so much responsibility, and she had to work hard just to feed us. Because she was getting no love, she had none to give. She had been an abused child herself.

She has remarried several times: the second man was gay; the third was an alcoholic and wife-beater; she and the fourth man stayed together for seven years; the fifth time, she married the third husband over again; her sixth marriage, a recent one, has lasted for two years.

As I mentioned before, on my return from my grandmother, I lived with Dad. I still loved my dad, but I was becoming mature, and his relationship with me underwent subtle changes. He treated me more like a wife than a child.

And then, all of a sudden, my grandmother, mother, and dad started accusing me of running around with boys and saying I would become pregnant before I was fifteen. That my dad would throw out stuff like that really hurt, even worse than my mother yelling at me for stealing what she had taught me to steal.

I hadn't been able to say that I was stealing for my mother because I would get another beating. I couldn't say that my dad was responsible for my sexy ways, either, because then I'd get taken away from him and sent back to my mother. Of all possible alternatives, living with her again was the maximum evil.

Although I was flirty, I never did anything really wrong. I picked up with a black boyfriend, and experimented with drugs. The time was the late '60s. The drugs then were pure, and we were not afraid to take them. But my dad did not approve of a boyfriend, and he started beating me too.

Then's when I began feeling suicidal. Nothing I could do worked. It was like banging my head against a brick wall. I began sniffing glue, anything to get high. Distinctions between reality and fantasy began to dim, and my grades in school took a downward dip.

Both the school and a social-service agency intervened. I was put in a group home. For the first time in my life, I thought, I'm getting a real chance. "God, don't let me muff it."

The group-home father was black, but the group was racially mixed. I think he wanted an all-black group, because I was framed and blamed for actions which I did not do. The group-home parents determined to get rid of me.

Because they were going to send me away, I tried to commit suicide. Then I was beaten up by the group-home father. I had had all I could take. I started fighting back. The police came, and they beat me up too, but not before I knocked one of them out badly enough to be hospitalized. I had never hated anyone before. Now I began to hate. I ran.

And on the run I was raped. So—at last—I had lost my virginity. The police caught me and put me in juvenile detention. I was either fourteen or fifteen years old.

One of the attendants in detention asked me to have sex with him. I refused. He said he would have me sent up forever. Absolutely beside myself with rage, fear, despair, I tried to set a fire. For that I spent a week with my hands tied behind my back, naked except for underclothing. From there I was transferred to the juvenile diagnostic center. Two housemothers there were kind to me, and one kept telling me that God loved me.

Love!

I didn't need any love.

All love had ever brought me was pain.

I was sent to the state school for girls.

I was put in the worst cottage. If two of us started fighting there, they put boxing gloves on us, and told us to finish it. We literally were made to scrub the floor with toothbrushes, and the humiliation of it was that the floor was clean to begin with. My hands and knees got raw.

Finally, Dad came to the rescue. He got me out on habeas corpus. He had discovered, someplace in the state, a Good Shepherd Home, and he had gone out and literally begged the nuns to take me. He brought me there on a pre-placement visit. That's when I met Sister Mary. She acted as though she would be glad to have me come, and she tried to make me realize that she had faith in me. This program, I knew, I *had* to make work. It offered my last chance.

But I was so angry, so hate-filled, that I was mean, ugly, and rude. I hated everybody and everything. I was one raging bundle of hatred.

My first confrontation came when a houseparent asked me to wash the floor. "No," I yelled, "that's your job!"

I pulled a can opener on her, threw the whole bucket of water over her, and then threw the bucket. I was bigger than she was, but she didn't even wince. "Angela," she said, "I love you. God loves you. Everyone here loves you." I just stared at her. And then I began to cry, big tearing sobs. That was the beginning of a turning point for me, but only a beginning.

I fought, over nothing much. I was angry. And I was in trouble most of the time.

As I said, I got into fights and all kinds of other problems. I couldn't seem to get along in the cottage living area at all. Besides, because I got into so much trouble, I also got blamed for things I didn't do. So I threw myself into school, stayed in school as much as possible, and tried to avoid people. People, for me, were bad news.

We had levels in group living, and with each level we moved into, we got more privileges. I couldn't get out of level 1, and I was sick of it. Level 1 was the Yellow Cottage. To this day, I hate yellow.

But I hung in there, and I didn't try to run for one whole year. Sister Mary was not my group mother, she was over all of them. But she always had an aura of love about her. She was compassionate. She had that crucial one-on-one touch.

Sister Mary is a lady.

A lady. That says it.

But I didn't show how much I appreciated her. Not yet. That would be risking entirely too much.

I did try to earn my way out of that Yellow Cottage.

One day some of the girls ran away, and a group of us ran after them with the intention of catching them and bringing them back. But of course we all ended up running.

Later on, I really did run.

I phoned my cousin, then in a high-falutin' sorority. I asked her to come get me and show me some fun. She took me back to the party she had already been in. They smoked grass and screwed in sleeping bags. I thought, "If that's what the good life is all about, I don't need it." I left and made my way back to the Good Shepherd Home.

The Good Shepherd Home and the Yellow Cottage.

I shouldn't have run, of course. I was placed in seclusion to think things over. My best girlfriend gave me the New Testament to read, so I had a kind of retreat. I thought, prayed, pondered the words, the message of God's love.

I remembered all the Sisters I had lived with: the Oblate Sisters to begin with; then the teaching Sisters when I was with my grandmother on my dad's side; and now the Good Shepherd Sisters. I recalled that when I left the one Catholic school I went to, Sister Evelyn had given me a small statue of Our Lady. Through all my moves and trials I had clung to that statue. I meditated over my instructions to become a Catholic. And I got a sense that maybe I was beginning to develop roots.

Not real roots, just tentative feelers.

Sister Mary started prayer groups. Of course, where Sister Mary went, I wanted to go if I could. I joined her prayer group. For me it was very meaningful. On the spiritual level with Sister Mary, I could relate. We shared something in common. Together we became born-again Christians or charismatic Catholics, or whatever one chooses to call it.

I did make it out of that Yellow Cottage. But not for long. Back I went again.

And then the time came for me to leave.

I'd like to say that my wounds were healed, but in fact, they had not as yet even been exposed. I had been hurt so much and so deeply that I was not yet ready to talk.

I was released to my dad, but I really wanted to be on my own. I had almost no school left to complete, so I finished that and worked two jobs at the same time. When I turned eighteen I said goodbye to Dad, loaded the car which I had bought, and moved into my own apartment.

I went, briefly, to California. While I was there, my father was shot.

A man came to the door, took aim, and fired. My father shot back in self-defense and hit his assailant. The police arrived.

My dad held the smoking gun. The police shot and killed him. The man who started the whole incident is still living.

I almost went berserk. My dad. The only member of my family who had loved and trusted me; who had always had faith in me. I ran, just ran blindly. Cross-country to New York. Back across the continent again to the West Coast. And then I headed for New York once more.

EIGHT

Corners Are Safe

A SEXUALLY abused child often responds to her feelings of helplessness and violation with a growing rage which can sometimes be hard to detect. The younger the child, the more completely the rage is suppressed. As she or he grows older, however, that anger aches to find adequate expression. It may propel the child into running away. If acted out it may show itself in clashes with authority: in the family, in school, or with the law. There have been instances reported in the last few years of children murdering their abusing parents.

Rage can also be directed inward; then it may manifest itself as depression, lethargy, psychiatric problems, suicide, or other forms of self-punishment.

The girls I worked with during my years as principal of Good Shepherd Schools had many reasons for anger other than sexual abuse. For a variety of reasons, they often displayed tremendous anger.

Once, when I had just come to a Home to take over the school, I was alone in the recreation room with, I suppose, eighty or so girls. I saw two of them getting into a hot argument, then physically fighting. I soon became aware that sides were being drawn. In a flash, I knew the whole eighty were going to get into a free-for-all, and once started, we might need the police to stop them.

Without thinking, I jumped between the two fighting girls. Had I stopped to think, I would never have done it; they didn't know me. I could easily have become a punching ball in the middle of the fight. But they stopped, and the two walked away in different directions, the whole fracas dissolved.

I saw another Sister do that once. Two girls were dishing out dessert in the kitchen for the evening meal, and I was sitting in the dining room with 150 teenagers. The girls got into an argument over the dessert. Suddenly one grabbed a carving knife and began chasing the other around the kitchen serving counter. The Sister cook, who was rather elderly, jumped in between them. That ended it.

Often I supervised study hour at night for 150 girls when I was the only adult present. They were divided up, studying in different rooms. Many of them did not want to be in the Home. Most of the girls were bigger and stronger than I and could easily have taken my keys without hurting me: one could have held me, another taken the keys, and they could all have run. For whatever reason, nobody ever, in my entire experience, touched or threatened me.

I remember one night when guests were present for a play put on by the girls. Two of the girls went out of control, furiously angry, and stormed out into an adjoining hall. Another Sister and I followed them and locked the doors at each end. The guests were horrified, especially the men, that we two Sisters were locked in with the angry teenagers. The men wanted to come in and help us, but the Sisters knew we were all better left alone.

The girls were very angry, not over anything that I can recall, just angry. I thought they would break the windows and jump out. They did make a few half-hearted attempts to do that, one tapping on the window with a high-heeled shoe. They were so furious that I expected them to smash up the furniture. I figured they were too angry to hear anything, so I kept still, but the other Sister kept up a conversation with them. In half an hour it was all over—the longest half-hour I ever want to live.

I always found openly expressed anger much easier to deal with than anger expressed in other ways. Some girls showed their anger by being sloppy, habitually late, careless, or indifferent. They didn't even realize that they were angry. Falling asleep was another exhibition of anger, sleeping through school or games or recreation.

Most of my life has been lived with teenage girls, and in my own mind I used to excuse such behavior because they were just growing up. In more recent years I have been absolutely amazed by the numbers of adults I see doing exactly the same things. For example, I've watched an adult who didn't get his or her way in some little thing in a social situation deliberately settle down to sleep, as though the person figured that was the best way of annoying everybody else.

Generally, the girls in Good Shepherd Homes liked school. Nevertheless, I was always alert for a sudden reaction: a wild flash of anger, a tumultuous outburst, an unprovoked attack on an innocent companion. Because I knew that these youngsters had numerous causes for their anger, I usually weathered the explosion, and let it pass without comment.

That the girls could go on a rampage and break every window in the area, we Sisters knew. We knew also that here and there, now and then, such things did happen. In my own personal experience, I seldom observed physically destructive anger beyond a girl smashing her fist, in a sudden rage, through a glass door or window, cutting herself in the process, or against a wall with enough force to leave a dent in the plaster. Possibly the girls were more likely to express anger by running away. (During most of my years, Good Shepherd Homes were closed—locked—institutions, gradually becoming open or selectively open from the early '60s on.)

I do recall two instances of girls attempting to set fires, another way of expressing rage.

We guarded matches carefully, aware of the dangers they might pose. One night, as I was sleeping in a room within the girls' dorm, one girl went to the lavatory, piled flammable materials together, and put her one match to it. None of us woke up, or even smelled the smoke. For whatever reason (we called it God's protection), the fire died out by itself. No damage was done.

On another occasion, as the girls were preparing for bed, one girl lit a torch she had made out of paper and cloth, again with her one and only match, and ran along the girls' beds, trying to set the bedspreads on fire. Everybody was scared to move. Again, no bedspread caught on fire, and the torch burned itself out.

As I have said, there was not much overt expression of anger in my own personal experience. This was due, I think, to the opportunity given the girls of working off steam in a most unlikely way.

Up until the '60s, states or counties seldom paid us more than a couple of dollars a day, if that much, for the girls they placed with us. The Homes in which I directed the schools operated commercial laundries, usually doing flatwork for the railroads. Girls sixteen and over spent three or four hours a day in the laundry.

Watching the girls at work, I often thought that they got rid of a lot of unexpressed anger as they cracked sheets, folded towels, and shook linen. And, at the same time, they had the satisfaction of knowing they were constructively engaged.

The superintendent of a boys' training school in a state which sent most of its girls to our Home, came to us once for an extensive visit. He wanted to observe every operation in the Home, and spent some hours in the laundry. He noted the soiled linen coming in and the sparkling clean going out. "In my school," he said, " the boys dig holes one day and fill them up the next, just for something to do.

"Here the girls turn out a finished product in which they can take pride."

That era has passed. Pullman uses little linen any more, and few people use trains. But as I ponder the constructive outlets we provided for rage, I do remember the laundry.

The laundry also made it possible for girls to stay with the Sisters until graduation from high school, something often too costly for states or counties to consider now. Most of the girls I taught decided to remain until they got a diploma in their hands. "Outside," as they so often said, "I'll never graduate." Those girls who had been sexually abused in their homes, therefore, never had to return to them.

Girls with low self-esteem and with too much guilt could stay with the Sisters, who respected and loved them, until they developed their own innate sense of worth.

We do not like to consider the possibility of sadism in parent-child relationships. It does exist, and I have come across too much of it. As I look back, in fact, I remember stories which girls told me that I absolutely could not believe. Now, I'm afraid they were telling me the truth.

When Sister Madonna told me of her successful efforts on behalf of one teenager, I was keenly interested.

Because children who have been physically abused for the sadistic pleasure of fathers or mothers need endlessly loving, one-on-one supportive treatment by adults, I want to present Sister Madonna's story here in her own words.

I became Penny's counselor.

For a social worker, a thirteen-year-old should not have proved too challenging.

After all, I could use behavior mod, or Rogerian techniques, or I could work with her under psychiatric direction.

I couldn't.

Penny challenged me past the latest therapeutic know-how. Past and beyond.

Her father had physically absued her. Seriously.

Penny's problems first surfaced in public school. A school psychologist discovered that her father had kept her tied to a pole in the basement. A pole with her name on it.

She hated her father. She loved her mother, she said, because her mother let her loose when her father was out of the house. But her mother *had* permitted the abuse.

And, in truth, Penny knew that. But she couldn't say it. The total rejection hurt too much.

Penny was disruptive in school. She fought.

A few months in a psychiatric hospital didn't help.

She went to an open residential treatment center—one in which patients have free access to come and go—and attended public school again.

More fights. Drugs, too.

The next step would be a state hospital. If that happened,

her mental-health worker said, she'd never get out. She'd be terminal. Warehoused there forever.

Our Good Shepherd Home, a partly closed residential-treatment center, took Penny. The staff were not hopeful, but her mental-health worker pleaded, "Give her one more chance."

So I got Penny.

First thing, Penny started fights, usually with other abused teenagers, aggressive like herself.

A child who has been hurt that much, that long, doesn't feel good when living goes right. Pain had been a constant in Penny's brief life. She courted it: tripped kids, stole, called names—anything to get beaten up. Then she cried and screamed, wept and wailed, but her anxiety level went down.

We talked.

Except during school hours, her dad had kept her tied up. During holidays, during the long summer days, he tied her up. She didn't know what normal living meant.

Fortunately, she was small. A big girl could have wrought a lot more destruction than Penny was capable of when her rage exploded. She wanted to rip every curtain, break every dish, scratch every face. I would put my arms around her and hold her tight until the wild fury subsided. Undernourished, probably, she had not yet reached puberty.

Did she know she was a girl?

Did she know the difference between boys and girls?

No.

She'd had a smattering of sex education in school. I gave her the rest. That meant long talks together when Penny was able to sit still more than fifteen minutes.

Penny knew about dogs. Her dad put two big dogs down in the basement with her. He didn't tie them; he only tied humans. Girl and dogs were abandoned there for hours.

When he released all three, the dogs were thirsty. So was she, of course, but the dogs came first. Dad heated water almost to the boiling point, and poured it into pans for the dogs. Eagerly, they rushed forward to lap it up—and then howled with the pain. Those dogs were all Penny had; she wept with them, fellow sufferers together.

Penny was bright, and she got the message: you're repeating the pain because you're used to it. She stopped fighting.

But she had to do something. So she hid. When the anxiety, the lack of pain, hit her too hard, she hid.

Our buildings were big, old, and rambling. They provided all kinds of nooks and crannies. Good hiding places. But Penny couldn't be left alone; she'd been left alone too long.

Whenever Penny disappeared, somebody searched until they found her. They didn't disturb her; she needed the space and time. But they told me where she was. I dropped whatever, whomever, and headed for the general area. Penny might be crouching beneath a chair or a desk or in a corner. Abused children like corners; they're safe. They don't hit, and they don't yell, and they don't tie people up. They shelter. And they can be gotten out of.

Gently, I'd let Penny know I was there. I'd say, "It's safe. When you're ready, I'm here." At first it took a long time for Penny to feel safe, a very long time. Gradually the time grew shorter, down to only a few minutes.

When she emerged—pale, teary, shaken—we'd talk. Over the months she learned that she could talk instead of hide.

She had dropped fighting; by slow degrees, hiding went too.

I always felt particularly concerned about the girls who turned their anger in upon themselves. They usually looked so sad and depressed and withdrawn that I would try to reach out to them with all the determination and consistency I could muster. I'll never forget one girl who asked another Sister to tell me that I was only wasting my time on her, and please to leave her alone because she wasn't any good and never would be; she wasn't worth my effort.

I responded by trying twice as hard to be kind and loving toward her, but she never responded. Not that it worried me too much. Some day, I thought, she'd begin wondering why I showed her so much love, and then maybe she'd find the answer: that she was a lovable person.

One girl spent an entire year in one of our schools and never spoke as much as one word to me. She was one of the quiet ones, always in a corner, never causing any trouble to anyone. But I kept trying, always saying a pleasant word when I met her. After she left, she wrote me one explosive letter after the other, with language far beyond the worst I had ever heard. She poured out pages and pages of boiling anger and rage; she accused the Sisters of all kinds of mistreatment. After she had expressed all the repressed anger and I had responded only with love, she asked to see me. We met in a place away from the Home. At our first meeting she brought a knife along and showed me how to throw it. We met many more times and eventually became good friends.

I remember Anna: beautiful, willowy, and long-legged, with lovely brown eyes and very white teeth. She starred in one of our school ballets. In that particular school I had been able to engage a professional ballet teacher; we could never have paid her adequately, so she donated her services. Anna loved her part and we were scheduled to give several performances.

I had talked extensively with Anna about her problem with self-mutilation, but she had never revealed any cause of underlying guilt. "Anna," I told her, "if you mutilate yourself during the performance of this ballet, I am going to take you out of it." The first performance was superb. Anna won congratulations and praise from everybody, but, not surprisingly, she couldn't handle the praise. I should have foreseen that. Before the second performance could take place, she had inserted a bead under her fingernail. Taking her out of the play killed me, but Anna accepted my decision stoically. She had never discussed her problems, and she was not going to do so now.

When not in school, Linda was kept tied to the bedpost in her room, kept there to be kicked or beaten or abused in whatever manner might occur to the abuser. All the family members who wished to could work out their anger by physically abusing the girl tied there for their pleasure.

She ate there, if she ate at all.

Linda came to us, a bright, pretty, intelligent girl. Her own sense of self-worth, of self-esteem, had been so bruised and battered that she no longer hoped for kindness or consideration. She had been so seriously deprived that she anticipated deprivation. She couldn't hope for good things for herself; to hope only meant to invite disappointment.

To have raged and fought against the injustices meted out to her would have brought Linda only further pain. She had no reason to expect anything other than pain. She assumed that her "badness" had caused her mistreatment, and she clung to that belief.

Linda couldn't accept our love or generosity, or the good

opportunities we tried to provide her with. Her self-defeating behavior was sad to observe. She had armored herself against our advances, and she dealt with her anger by attributing it to us: Sisters, girls, whoever was around.

If this sounds confused, it was. In simple language, Linda was accepting the deprived world she had inhabited, and she embraced the deprivation.

We had to ask that Linda be transferred to a treatment center better equipped to deal with her special problems than we could.

Of the girls and women who are telling their stories throughout this book, Angela and Rosemary were actively acting out their anger before and during their placement in a Good Shepherd Home. Marcie couldn't do that; she was depressed and cried a lot, but she also talked at length with the one Sister she loved. Iris withdrew at first when she entered the Home, but conformed outwardly. Pearl's life was marked for years by a profound depression.

Angela and Rosemary each needed a year; Iris took eighteen months; Pearl had not yet dealt with the real problem after eight and a half years of therapy; and Marcie did not really find the strength to confront the full force of her anger until some years after she had left the Good Shepherd Home.

I've known women to contact me twenty years after they left the Home, having never written or phoned in between, to tell me that they were now prepared to deal with the trauma of childhood sexual abuse, and to ask for my help.

As I have already pointed out, seldom did I know that some girls in the Good Shepherd Homes had been sexually abused until after they had left, established themselves, and then found the courage to visit, phone, or write to me about the problem. Other girls among the groups with which I worked undoubtedly talked to whichever Sisters they had developed confidence in. Probably some of them, now grown women, have never yet discussed or resolved their difficulties arising from sex abuse. Only after a girl's anger, suspicion, and fear have been allayed, at least in part, can treatment become effective.

That can take a long time.

NINE

Iris

MY DIFFICULTIES began with the death of my mother when I was two years old and my brother was just six weeks. Soon after that, my father, a farmer, married his divorcée housekeeper with two small children of her own. When I was six years old my stepbrother, age five, became ill. As was the usual routine, it was my turn to stay in from the fields, tend to household chores, meals, and, this time, to administer a medication that was prescribed for his illness. The boy died within a week.

From that day on I became the "poisoner" and "murderer," living with daily and nightly taunting, and mocking re-enactments of my "crime."

My brother and I became objects of *gross* child abuse. We were severely beaten, denied food and clothing, and we slept with the animals. We were bound and gagged in the attic or basement for days at a time. We were subjected to sexual atrocities and torture by our stepmother. My father, seemingly oblivious, never made any attempt to stop it or to help us. Naked and starving, shorn of our hair, we began running away, stealing barn coats from neighboring porches for both cover and warmth. Each time we ran we were returned to our home by the police. The police did not question us, and I never told.

From age six to eight I lived like this and took what care I could of my brother, who was only a baby.

Finally, when I was eight, our country school teacher risked her reputation and her job in a personal effort and crusade to get the courts to remove us permanently from our circumstances. She was successful (and was also fired for causing so much trouble), and my baby brother and I were placed in a series of separate nearby foster homes. Because I loved my father and did not blame him, but only my stepmother, for the physical and sexual abuse, I ran away from each foster home and returned home. I always hoped that *this* time my father would show his love and take care of us.

He never did.

Then I was placed in a distant and, looking back, a very fine foster home. I responded with resentment and belligerence to every effort at kindness and generosity. I would not make friends, truanted from school, lied and deceived, stole household money, and finally began shoplifting.

So I came to the Good Shepherd Home.

For eighteen months I was introverted and detached. I didn't know where my brother was, nobody ever wrote or came to see me. The Sisters' words or presence made no impression. My caseworker, the only link to my family, only added to my inner turmoil. I was too far away from home to consider running away, so I conformed outwardly, did well in school, took part in activities when I had to. But I never smiled, never tried to make friends. I thought of myself as evil and ugly.

Then one day an incident occurred which changed everything. Sister Daniel had intercepted a letter I had written to my father, telling him where I was and asking that he come and take me home. Alone in her office, I was shattered at her intrusion into my very private thoughts and also somewhat ashamed. I began defending my action and repeating the dream which I had run after for so long: that my father loved me. Suddenly, I heard myself pouring out my real feelings. Never in my life had I expressed them to anybody.

Sister Daniel took me into her arms, held me tight, and let me cry. I cried and cried until I could cry no more.

Sister said that she could not answer the questions which puzzled me so, but that she did know that God loved me, and she loved me. Indeed, she said, she loved me very much and wanted me to be happy. She explained that I had not come to the Home for punishment. Never for punishment. She said I had come for healing, for learning how to accept love as well as give love, so that I could later on make a happy life for myself.

Then, in an offhand way, Sister remarked that I reminded her of another classmate, whom I admired because she was pretty, popular, and trusted with responsibility, and who came and went at will in the Home.

For the first time since my mother died I heard nice, good, positive things being said about *me!*

At that moment I became a person.

I understood and related to words such as "capable" and "potential," and related to them as spoken about me. I accepted Sister's judgement. Above all, I *believed* I could be like that other girl, simply because Sister said so.

With my defenses down and barriers removed, I spent three more wonderful years at the Home, years of transformation and personal and spiritual growth and development. I made friends, learned new skills, discovered my talents and special interests. I asked for and got trust and responsibility. I learned the qualities of self-determination and self-reliance and initiative. I wanted to make the Home a better place just because I was in it.

I became the leader of a crew of girls who, for nothing more than the privilege of singing at the top of our lungs, or for extra midday and evening snacks, would scrub and refinish floors, paint walls, wash windows, sew new curtains, refinish worn furniture—all with a minimum of supervision. We were on our own and we loved it.

I excelled on the sewing machine and would mend and sew new dresses for girls who needed them. In my spare time I would sew pajamas, aprons, and other items which we would sell on visiting days. I developed an interest in the business world and in publications in particular. I started a school paper and resurrected our long-dormant yearbook. I got my first job as a part-time secretary in the city. By the time I graduated, I had been riding in high gear for some time.

TEN

Just Listen

BEFORE the treatment of a sexually abused adolescent can begin, she must have established a relationship of some trust with whatever person will be working with her.

For the sexually abused girl, that relationship is a difficult one. She has been tricked and fooled and used and taken advantage of by so many people for so long that she is totally and justifiably suspicious of all adults.

Perhaps Catholic girls might tend to have some sense of trust in Catholic Sisters. However, the vast majority of the girls I worked with were not Catholics. They belonged to a variety of denominations or, in most cases, they belonged to none, had not been attending church, and did not pray. They knew nothing about nuns. Their first order of business was to figure out who and why we were. The period of testing us went on longer than it might have under other conditions.

To guide me, I had the directions given us by Sister Euphrasia Pelletier, who founded the Order of the Good Shepherd in 1835. She left a book of instructions for those of us working with girls and women who had been victims of society. I selected the three points which seemed most pertinent, and stuck to them like glue.

Sister Euphrasia said that she wanted written in words of gold and hung on every convent wall this admonition: *Never, never strike a girl.* That stringent rule might seem obvious until one has tried working with a girl who trusts nobody and who tests everybody to the limits of their endurance. Dealing with withdrawn, suspicous adolescents is, at the least, challenging; it can become agonizing and frustrating.

Love the girls, Sister Euphrasia said. Love them very much. In the long run, I think almost all of the girls eventually recognized that love which we tried to give them, asking for nothing back. I remember Anna whom I have mentioned before—the teenager I took out of the ballet because of her self-mutilation.

She chose to stay at the Home until she graduated from high school. Years and years passed; I never heard from her. Then one night, perhaps twenty years after we had said good-bye, a long-distance phone call came. "This is Anna. Do you remember me?"

I certainly did.

She went on to describe her current life. She was an anchorwoman for the evening edition of the local news at one of the network affiliates in a big city, and she was studying law because she wanted to become an international lawyer. She loved travel, and that looked like a good way to see the world and work at the same time.

"How did you ever find me?" I asked, for I had changed both my name and location. (I had been Sister Dominic, my father's name, but after he died I changed back to Vera, my own name, because I got so tired of explaining to people why I had a man's name.)

"I phoned all over the country," she said.

Then she explained why she had called. "I was feeling lone-some, and I tried to think whether even one person in my whole life had loved me just for myself. That's when I re-membered you." Anna talked for a long, long time that night. She has not phoned since. I hope that means that she has found her peace.

The third prescription I took from Sister Euphrasia is very simple: *Just listen.* As one older Sister told me in my youth: "You don't have to say a word; just listen and nod once in a while." Very seldom before placement with us had the girls found any adult who would listen to them. The adults they knew generally had too many problems of their own.

In the case of sexual abuse, the youngster needs to talk about it at length, to repeat the story over and over until the rankling, bitter memories have been purged. In their per-sonal accounts one can see that each girl eventually tells her story again and again; each seems compelled to repeat and re-repeat the sordid details to a friend she has come to know over a long period, a friend who is trusted, receptive, em-pathetic, and tireless.

I have already begun Sister Madonna's story of her long slow progress in treating Penny, who had spent most of her young life tied to a pole in her father's basement. Penny learned, eventually, neither to hide nor to fight; she discov-ered that her anger could be talked out.

In Sister Madonna's words:

Penny had to see me right away whenever she needed to; otherwise she panicked. "Whenever Penny wants to see me," I told the staff, "get me."

She needed to see me often. She had to make sure that I

would really be there, that I really would talk to her, that I really would not tie her up in the basement and leave her there with two dogs.

She didn't know. How *could* she know?

In my office once, she saw a roll of masking tape on my shelf. She stiffened. "What's that for?"

"For my door. I want to put up a schedule."

"Only for your door?

"Sure it's for your door?

"I hate it!"

She got upset, really uptight.

"What do you know about tape, Penny?"

Tears. Sometimes her father would stuff a sock in her mouth and then tape her mouth shut with masking tape.

Oh, my child. My child. Why did you suffer so?

Gently, I removed the tape.

How much else lay buried in one small memory? How much more lay hidden, unconscious, to affect her life?

I often gave Penny a surprise. We took a walk and stopped at a Dairy Queen. Why? No why, no reason. Bad things happen without *whys*. Good things happen without *whys*, too.

I visited every girl's room at night and blessed her with a prayer. Some nights I dropped a candy bar on Penny's pillow or left a bottle of pop. Life could have rules: bad things come unearned, but good things come unearned, too.

Penny wanted to phone home fairly often. She felt guilty about her family. She had been blamed for every misfortune that befell the family and she still felt responsible.

Were they doing all right?

As well as could be expected with a family where every child—as soon as he or she reached fifteen—runs away from home.

As well as parents and children can do when, every now

and then, all the children are locked in the basement without food because the mother is an author, and when her literary friends drop in she does not want children bothering her genius and interfering with her talent.

As well as can be expected when the children, hungry and securely locked, can hear the party and celebrating and drinking going on upstairs.

Penny felt that she ought to go back and visit and make sure that her family was okay.

She and I phoned her parents for permission.

No, they said. Her bed had been sold.

All the teens at the Home went out together now and then on a trip or an excursion or for skating or bowling. Penny and I phoned to ask her parents if she might go with the rest. (The Home always clears outside trips with parents.)

No, they said, she needed punishment. No rewards for Penny. They forbade it.

What to do? Her mental-health worker and I wrote trips into her treatment plan and got them approved by her supervisor. Heaven knows, Penny needed them, if only for socialization.

Penny would have nothing to do with white men. Understandable enough. Black staff had treated her well at the psychiatric hospital, and now she was convinced that only black men could be trusted.

"Not all," I tried to say; "not all. You judge each person individually, no matter what color."

How does one begin at the bottom of life experiences and impart all of them to a girl who is thirteen, and fourteen, and fifteen? How does one figure out which spaces are empty? How can one teach a teen what she ought to have acquired unconsciously as a toddler?

I took the place of Penny's mother, told her all those things a mother should have told her years ago.

She didn't know how to look pretty, didn't know how to dress. We looked at catalogs together, studied women's faces, talked about hair styles, selected clothes for various occasions. Penny learned fast. From looking like some poor bimbo on the streets, she began to look like a New York model. "That's too far the other way, Penny. School girls don't look like you look now."

Sometimes, during counseling sessions, Penny would scream at me, and I'd scream back at her. (This was a couple of years after we began and she was coming to trust me.) Then we'd talk about it, and what it felt like. All mothers scream sometimes and Penny needed to know that. And I'd point out that she could change our direction at any time by calming down, using a normal voice, and discussing the subject.

So many, many things to teach.

Holidays were hard for Penny. Often, they're tense for all of us, but for abused children they're worse. They have no memory of good times when everybody else is celebrating. Girls who couldn't go home for the holidays were likely to be unwanted and probably abused. I'd stay up with them for forty-eight hours straight.

I wanted to give them traditions, something to remember a holiday by. So we'd do something crazy, like eating dessert first. We'd go off the grounds to some place with really good desserts, and every girl would have whatever she wanted. And then we'd go to a movie or the park or for a walk, and after that we'd eat dinner. Later, I'd hear one of them say, "Holidays are really weird; we always eat dessert first." It gave them something to associate with holidays.

Along the way, I encouraged Penny's talents, praised her

good grades, and went to her school functions. I became her family. She had no other, nobody else.

Penny stayed at the Home for three and a half years, moving gradually through all the levels: the group home on the grounds; off the grounds with supervision; and finally into an apartment of her own.

Penny will soon graduate from the professional school which she has attended for two years. Whenever I go through her town, I visit her. We talk. Sometimes she phones. My hanging in there makes her feel special. And indeed she is: a very special young woman.

Penny is making it.

Good Shepherd Sisters have set up several shelters for battered women in the U.S. Visiting them, I've learned that, along with patient and supportive care, the Sisters have developed a wide array of services.

In one city in the midwest, the Sisters have a preliminary requirement that a woman who is at that time being beaten up, leave the batterer and leave him without letting him know where she will be. The Sisters suggest that women and children stay at the shelter for ninety days, but this is flexible. If they need to, women and children can stay longer at the shelter; if, on the other hand, they can make adequate arrangements for themselves elsewhere in less time, they can do that.

According to Sister Pauline, the Sisters give the women help, should they need it, to apply for public assistance, and to get court orders for protection from their abusers. The women are encouraged to save their welfare funds for the day when they leave the shelter: "We state a nominal charge of one dollar a day for the women, and fifty cents a day for each child, but seldom collect it. Within the past year I doubt that we were paid as much as a total of one hundred dollars altogether by the women."

The Sisters provide shelter, food, and whatever other necessities are called for. A preschool has been set up on the grounds for small children during the morning hours; older boys and girls can go to a public school only a block from the shelter. The Sisters make sure that those women and children who need medical care because of the beatings get whatever assistance is required.

Psychologist Lenore Walker points out that children of battering fathers—boys in particular—develop that abusive pattern in their own attitude toward women, beginning with their mothers. I have seen boys as young as four threatening their mothers and striking out at them. To help break this pattern, the Sisters seek men to become involved in the living group and preschool, to demonstrate respect for women, and to serve as adult male role models for the little girls, who are automatically frightened when a man does as much as walk into a room.

In this particular city, a network of social workers has been developed. Catholic Charities, a Neighborhood House, and the Salvation Army all provide caseworkers who assist the women on an individual basis. Additionally, the Sisters have engaged a social worker. For group therapy for the battered women, the YWCA provides a group worker, and the Salvation Army provides another.

This shelter can accommodate as many as fourteen women with children. Says Sister Pauline, "We still have to refuse, for lack of space, more women than we accept. The need for shelter for battered women is critical."

The Good Shepherd Sisters find the resources needed to operate the shelter in whatever ways they can: grants, contributions, government surplus food, and any money-making efforts they can dream up.

In another area, in the southwest, the Sisters operate a shelter with slightly different arrangements. They have purchased an apartment building so that each woman with children has her own apartment. They ask the battered women to stay with them for nine months, if that is possible. And they have built a school on their grounds so the children can get an education right there.

Meanwhile, the women are also encouraged to attend school, where they learn such skills as sewing, cooking, and budgeting. Again, they get help in applying for welfare, and they are advised to save as much of this money as possible for the day when they leave to establish themselves in independent living.

An after-care worker is also on the shelter staff. In this shelter the after-care worker is Pearl, who will tell her own story in Chapter 13. The position means a great deal to Pearl because she once had so little confidence in her own abilities and didn't think she could ever get a job. When I mentioned Pearl's joy to the administrator, she replied, "We are as concerned about helping those whom we employ as we are about the specific population we serve."

These services are always free of charge. As usual, the Good Shepherd Sisters hunt for money wherever funds can be obtained.

As I observed the quality of caring given to battered women and frightened children at the various shelters, I was impressed by the love and respect that the Sisters give, always on a very personal basis, to each woman and child in the shelter. In such an atmosphere, women who have felt degraded and unloved can tentatively begin their long journey toward inner healing. Finally, Sisters are always available for that service most urgently needed of all: listening. Women can talk at length, children can play with joy and can also tell their stories to the Sisters, confident that they will give them the time, and that they will care.

"What helped you the most?" I asked one young woman.

I had expected that she would mention the freedom from worrying about getting the essentials for herself and her two small children, or the time given to help her get over the trauma, or even a sewing or cooking class.

She smiled. "What helped me most was what the Sisters showed me about God: that he is real, that he is always working in my life, that he loves me, that he is a God of gentleness and peace.

"I was raised in a religion which presented God as a judge; he was a strict and stern God whom I struggled always to please, without ever getting the sense that I had succeeded. In a way I was rebelling against that God when I married my husband; my husband was unpredictable and exciting and cast in a different mold, I thought.

"In the end, of course, I had selected a man cast in the image of my God—that image which I know now to be false. I had chosen a man who was stern and strict, who could never be pleased, and who punished me by beatings.

"Believe me, that won't happen twice."

I've seen the kinds of treatment the Sisters offer to those young or older women in their care who are burdened with addiction to drugs or alcohol.

Before they come to a transition home in an eastern city, the addicted women have completed a medically supervised drying-out period. They come to the home to recover, get themselves established, form addiction-free habits, complete their education, and obtain employment.

The Sisters are present to listen, encourage, motivate, and support women while they are in the process of getting plugged back into everyday activities and life.

I noticed some striking and quite unusual paintings around that Home. They were done by a young woman who had never known that she had any artistic ability, and who had never before attempted to draw or paint anything. She was shyly pleased when I complimented her on the paintings; she said she may go on to a career in commercial art. The Sisters put the women in touch with vocational rehabilitation programs, and provide the incentives for them to study those skills in which they may be competent.

A couple of women were completing secretarial courses in business college; some were working for their L.P.N. degrees in nursing; another was aiming to prepare herself for a position in commerical selling, and told me that she would be going for an interview the next day—the number of applicants for that particular position had been screened down to five, and she was one. Some women completed college and earned undergraduate degrees while with the Sisters.

Unless a woman is actually holding a job, no money is asked for by the Sisters at this transition home; should she obtain work, the fee requested is minimal. Time spent with the Sisters is flexible and is determined by each woman's need.

When I asked one woman who had been addicted to alcohol and other drugs what had helped her most she replied, "Somebody is always here to listen to me; any time I want to talk, I can find a Sister to talk to. In my life, that situation had never existed before."

In another Home in the U.S., the Sisters accept women from prison who were sentenced for nonviolent crimes. If these women choose, they can spend the time of their sentences with the Sisters. There are no locks and no confinement. The women can use the time constructively to prepare themselves for some kind of employment, or they can get jobs if they are qualified.

Some of the women who have come here have been prostitutes. Some are bag ladies, or simply women who, because of some misfortune, are without home and funds. They could also be in shock after a particularly harrowing divorce.

Good Shepherd Sisters work with prisoners in several ways: they provide half-way houses for women on parole or work release; do casework in prisons; or accept women prisoners as an alternative to serving time.

Sister Thelma has been working in prison programs. Right now she is spending a year researching alternatives to prison.

As a caseworker, she has served the long-termers, women with years-long sentences. She has given them her own caring love, talked throughout the state to any group who would listen to her about the special needs of women prisoners, and raised funds to make their living conditions more tolerable. She has spurred church groups of various denominations to volunteer their services to women prisoners, to visit them, to deal compassionately with released women, and to get involved in social programs designed to keep women out of prison. She has found volunteers to teach reading and other skills to imprisoned women who needed such help, and to prepare women for their G.E.D. exam so that they would at least leave prison with high school diplomas. She has worked to get women into college on released time, arranging for women to attend college while still in prison. She has struggled to hold families together while the women were in prison.

According to Sister Thelma, a substantial number of women in prison have been sexually abused in childhood, but "They seldom talk about that." Sister helped one such woman to get an education while in prison; the woman has now completed her second year in graduate school for a master's in social work. With her degree, that woman will try to find work in a position in which she also can help women prisoners. "If only she can make it the rest of the way," says Sister Thelma. "She doesn't have the money to pay for school, and she doesn't have any way of getting funds."

The poor, the exploited, the oppressed, the abused need, most of all, people who respect their human dignity, listen to them, and love them.

The most important gift any abused child or adult can be given is personal, caring love given freely and without cost.

When I was working at St. Patrick's parish in Seattle, I initiated, along with an ecumenical St. Vincent de Paul Society, several services for the poor, the exploited, and the oppressed.

Actually, my first effort in the parish was the organization of a committee to promote social justice. I had come to realize that while we struggled to change the system, people were dying of hunger and cold; I worked to set up a variety of direct services.

To keep these operating we had some 400 to 500 volunteers from churches of all denominations. Several of them were outstanding in the numbers of hours they donated to the poor. One of these was Sally.

And then Sally told me her story.

Because she struggled so hard, for so long, and really determined her own healing and treatment, Sally's story is best told here:

Even as a child I was willful, determined, and independent. Recently my father told me that I couldn't be controlled.

I recall that as a teenager I began to experience bad dreams. A repetitive dream was of falling, falling, falling, and then jumping awake with my heart pounding and my head spinning. I remember dreaming about being cast in a junior high school play. At one point I wanted to scream in terror, but couldn't no matter how hard I tried. Besides all that, I felt angry all the time. No reason. I was just angry. Throughout my life, up to the age of thirty-seven I was an angry person.

I was a superachiever too. By age twenty-three I was in charge of all the prop work for a professional theater complex of three theaters. I have also held extremely important, sensitive and vital positions in civil service.

In high school I rarely dated. Actually, I was desperate to date and I regularly had crushes on all the cute boys, but I wasn't very successful at it. I was a shy, awkward teenager who found it easy to relate to boys academically, but not on a date. Boys wanted to neck, and that much physical contact made me feel very uncomfortable.

Besides, I had a strange idea that it was my responsibility to date guys I wasn't attracted to. It wasn't their fault, I reasoned, that they were unappealing. I envied those friends who had steady boyfriends. I wanted steadies, too, but I just couldn't do that. Not going to my senior prom hurt, but only guys I didn't like invited me, and I had finally figured out that it was okay to refuse them.

College, I thought, would give me a chance to start over and learn how to be popular. It was one long nightmare. If a man made any attempt to touch me or kiss me goodnight I got scared, as though the situation would get out of hand and I wouldn't be able to stop it. Now I can see that the guys were just doing what guys thought they were supposed to do: inviting me down to the riverbank for a little innocent necking. But I couldn't handle it. Because I couldn't figure out how to handle the physical side of a relationship, I dated and broke up with two really nice guys in the first month of school.

With the trauma of dating using up so much of my energy, I did not get the A's I could so easily have rated.

Despite all my feelings of ineptitude, I met a nice guy who was willing to accept my reticence about sex. We dated for four years, and then we got married. Recalling how terrified I felt, I'm amazed I went through with the wedding. I did, in fact, call it off once because I felt so frightened of losing my independence and freedom, and of conforming to somebody else's expectations. I remember telling my husband, "Don't expect me to change. I'll always be independent."

I remember having the strangest dreams after my marriage. I was standing in my family's driveway and somebody grabbed me from behind. Very calmly I would say, "Mother, Daddy, come and help me; someone's trying to hurt me."

Marriage was a lot more difficult than dating. I tried to have a good sexual relationship, but I couldn't understand why I felt such intense rage when my husband touched me, or why I didn't seem to recognize him when he looked down at me in bed.

My husband and I were committed. Both of us struggled to make our marriage work. But after eight years we had to realize that our marriage had failed. We separated. Having been friends before marriage, we wanted to continue our friendship, and have done so.

While working in the civil service in Washington, D.C., I decided to get into therapy. We'd been married a year then, a rough year, and my husband told me that I seemed angry at the world. He suggested that I might want to talk to someone. A good idea, but scary.

That something was fundamentally wrong with my sex life had not occurred to me. Or perhaps it had, but I doubted that anything could be done about it. Masters and Johnson and all the rest had not yet appeared on the horizon, so I didn't have a clue as to what might be wrong. I did not enter therapy, therefore, for problems with sex. I went because, in addition to my anger, I felt so sad. I'd come home from work and sit under the stereo headphones for hours trying to shut out my feelings of misery.

After one and a half years in therapy, I switched to psychoanalysis in an effort to get at the root of my problems. By then, I was just *beginning* to admit that the basic problem was sex. I worked with a wonderful analyst for over four years. Although I never got to the core of the problems which had plagued me for years, other matters did start falling into place. I came to trust my feelings implicitly and to know that I had reasons, hidden though they might be, for my behavior. Nothing I did was arbitrary.

Throughout treatment I was plagued with dreams of being suffocated and slowly strangled by men.

By the time we agreed that I should terminate treatment, we had both come to believe that I had been sexually abused, but we had no idea who, where, or what. I remember my analyst saying, "You may need to figure this out on your own." I responded by remarking on my stubborness.

I'm grateful to him for teaching me to trust my feelings. Because I still felt that something more had to be figured out.

In fact, I had lots of unsolved problems.

I found it hard to relate to women and rarely had more than one close woman friend. At work I delegated poorly, if at all. I always felt, without any specific reason, that people would let me down if I counted on them. Since none of us is perfect, I had lots of examples to prove this point.

After the divorce I dated occasionally, but I still wasn't good at it. I want to get married again, and throughout the ten years since my divorce I've dated some wonderful men, a couple for long periods of time. Two of them asked me to marry them; I actually did get engaged to one, but it didn't work out.

Although physical closeness was less terrifying, occasionally I still ended up crying, and once heard myself screaming, "Don't, *No.* Don't. No, don't do that." But I had no idea what I was talking about. Certainly I had improved since the days of my marriage, but I had not improved enough.

I had an interesting way, I realized, of choosing men who made me feel small and protected. I also selected men who either were or had the potential of abusing me.

Each one did care for me, and each contributed to my learning in some way. But I thank God that I did not marry any of them.

Several years after my divorce, I took part in a Human Potential training session. One assignment was designed to help participants discover what they wanted out of life. I thought I knew: home, husband, family. But the leader kept encouraging me to reach deep into myself to learn what I really did want. Suddenly, to my surprise, and through my tears, I heard myself cry out: "My *mom!* I want my *mom.*"

I felt as though somebody had cracked a raw egg open right in the middle of my chest, and incredible feelings gushed out. I fought and kicked, trying to get away from the man who was working with me, pulling him and the chair he was sitting in right across the floor. Thank God my partner was a paramedic, and he knew that I was doing only what I needed to do, and that he should stay with me without interfering. I remember hearing myself scream, "Don't!" Then I ended up in a little heap on my partner's lap, sobbing.

"Don't!"

Don't what?

I didn't know.

Perhaps, I thought, this had to do with a frightening hospital incident which I had experienced as a child, but I didn't know. My partner contacted me later to ask whether I had figured out what the "Don't" was all about. "No," I answered, and mentioned the hospital incident. He looked at me and slowly shook his head: "I think you were raped, Sally." Even as he spoke those words I found myself thinking, "Maybe you're right."

I had planned on visiting my family, and this seemed a good time to go. Perhaps they would know something.

I certainly needed to find out, because the strange feeling of dizziness which had enveloped me in my teenage dreams began creeping into my waking time. That dizziness seemed to have some relation to whatever had happened to me.

Not wanting to upset my mom with tales of sexual abuse, I asked her instead if she could remember whether I had ever fallen and hit my head, or had been seriously hurt in some way which would account for that awful dizziness. My mom couldn't think of anything, and concluded by explaining that she and my dad had rarely left me alone.

Right then she stopped talking as though she had stumbled

on something as she searched through her memory. Well, she said slowly, one time she and my dad had left me for a couple of hours. I had been asleep and she had asked the wife of the couple living downstairs (they owned the house we were renting) to look in on me.

I remembered the wife and the daughter, but could not recall any husband. Somewhat hesitantly I asked, "Did she have a husband?"

"Why, yes. Don't you remember him? His name was Tom. He was tall with dark hair, a young man, but kind of strange."

I didn't remember him, so my mother continued. He had suffered a number of minor strokes which had left him mentally confused. He talked but didn't make sense, laughed at nothing, and, although partially paralyzed on the left side of his face and body, he was very strong. He was also unpredictable. My mother told me about him grabbing her wrist one day when she was outside hanging up the laundry. Although she had managed to wriggle free, he had scared her. Mom said that his wife, Ruth, was trying to keep him at home rather than have him institutionalized, probably in a nursing home. (In fact, he was institutionalized and died in a nursing home six months later.)

Mom also remembered that Ruth, his wife, had told her and my dad when they returned that night that I had awakened very frightened after a bad dream; that she had comforted me, and that I had gone back to sleep. Because I seemed all right the next morning, they thought no more of the incident.

I recall every syllable of that conversation with my mother. As she was talking, I became more and more uneasy and scared. I reached across to her, and asked her to take my hand. Then I remember saying to her, "Oh, my God! Oh, my God!" and then I began crying, struggling, and fighting against the memory of the person who had hurt me. I remember my mom coming to me and holding me while I sobbed and sobbed. It looked as though I had discovered the *who;* now I needed to know *what* had happened.

Next morning I talked to my dad about all the feelings in my body and the emotions, but I had no picture of what had taken place. At that time, I had been two and a half years old. We discussed the misconception that bad memories will just "go away." My dad was amazed that a child so young could remember so much.

After those few days with my parents I thought that the nightmare from the past was over, but during the succeeding months I was troubled several times by the memory. Little pieces of the incident continued to come back, always when I was with close friends, people who were letting me know that they cared about me. With the memory always came the words, "No, *don't!* No, *don't!*" Then I would feel as though my face was being stretched tight, and I couldn't talk or yell. Often I would cough and choke. Gradually I began to remember that the weird young man downstairs had forced me into oral sex. I couldn't breathe and couldn't scream and had thought I was going to die. Then I had passed out. First I had fought as well as I could, but the young man was much too strong for me. I had yelled for help, but nobody came.

It seems to me that his wife must have discovered he was missing and found him after he had assaulted me. I have strange memories of some woman trying to comfort me, but she had been the wrong person. I remember, also, being stood in the bathtub while someone cleaned me off.

I didn't need to go back into psychoanalysis, that much was clear. I knew what happened, but I needed to deal with my feelings—lots and lots of feelings.

I recalled that my brother had been involved in peer coun-

seling during his years in the southwest. Peer counseling is
based on the philosophy that each individual knows exactly
what to do to keep her or himself emotionally healthy. All we
lack is the knowledge of how to take care of ourselves in the
way we need to. According to this philosophy, the people involved are allowed and encouraged to vent feelings, cry,
shake with fear, and so on. Such channels are a person's normal, instinctive way of healing the hurts she has suffered, but
most of us have been told not to do these things. Such stric-
tures come from well-meaning people who have never allowed themselves to deal with their own hurts.

I phoned my brother. He thought I would work well in
peer counseling and gave me the names of a couple of people
to contact. I couldn't find an available class on how to become
an effective peer counselor for another person, and I wasn't
willing to wait around, so I located a social worker trained in
this method. I saw her as a therapist. Three months later I
registered in a class for peer counseling.

Thus was initiated the journey of discovery and healing of
the hurt inflicted on me so many years ago. The unexplained
feelings began to make sense, as did the child who couldn't be
controlled. Of course not. She would never again allow herself
to be in anyone's power. She would be independent. It would
be difficult for her to delegate authority, to allow the outcome
of events to get out of her control. Physical closeness with
men would be painful and would inadvertently disturb the
buried memory. She would, unconsciously, be attracted to
men who were in one way or another abusive.

I had to deal with these feelings. Those unconscious repressed feelings of the two-and-a-half-year-old child had powerfully influenced my behavior throughout my life.

I worked through the feelings by stages: first the grief and sadness of being hurt and having nobody there to protect me; the murderous rage because someone had dared to violate me; the fear, the extraordinarily intense fear; and, finally, the delight and wonder that my body is really mine to decide what to do with, and when. It was truly amazing to me that merely saying, "This is *my* body," was enough to bring tears of joy.

I have been involved in peer counseling for a number of years now. The social worker has been replaced with a non-professional like me, and the changes in our lives have been incredible. I am now going with a man whom I love and trust, and we are talking in terms of marriage. And I am studying for a Ph.D. in counseling.

The sexual abuse of a very small child is insidious because so young a child tends to repress it. The only way I could have survived the experience was by thrusting it down deep into my memory where only the longing for intimacy could eventually shake it loose. My parents never knew. Even had I not repressed the memory, how could a two-and-a-half-year-old have found the words to describe the experience and the feelings it aroused?

To dismiss something like this in a small child as a bad dream is to take the easy way out. That child, grown to an adult, must be willing to trust herself, to believe that every behavior has a reason, as she searches out the *whys* of inexplicable actions and "funny" feelings.

My parents gave me the gifts of an abiding faith in a good God, and an insatiable curiosity. I never believed that God meant my life to be awful, and I was sure there was a reason for my feelings. I was determined to figure out why I didn't act and feel as others did. There have been moments, large moments, when I wondered which is worse: not knowing or dealing with the now-remembered feelings. Hard as it has been, I believe the struggle has been worth it, every minute of it. I would rather be me than anybody else in the whole world.

ELEVEN

Rosemary, Again

THE judge knew I had lied in court about my dad. He knew my dad had sexually abused me. So he said that I was going to the Good Shepherd Home.

Good Shepherd Home!

So *I* was the one who was going to be punished.

My first day at the Home was filled with surprises. Sister Gertrude met me with a gracious kindness. I had expected to meet a hard-faced, frustrated old nun who, being disappointed in love, had turned into a supposed servant of God. But Sister Gertrude was lovely. I was scared, withdrawn, depressed, and suspicious of everybody. Because Sister Gertrude was nice, I figured she was being kind to get information out of me. She was not going to get any.

I was given a uniform which I hated immediately. The girls stared at me. I wanted to slap the faces of every one of them.

The second, third, and fourth weeks I thought I'd die. But I wouldn't admit it. I could hold my head up high and tell everyone who crossed me where to go.

I could do well in school, and good work was expected. I

decided to do everything as well as possible for the principal, Sister Vera. I suspected that maybe, just maybe, I might have found a friend. I was scared of that feeling.

I couldn't keep my temper under control, and kept fighting with everyone.

I felt despondent and blue. I cried often to myself. I was happy only in class with Sister Vera. But I was afraid to let her know that I liked her.

I was too angry and too hurt to change my behavior, or even to talk about it. One day I took aim, and flung my book at a teacher. Another day I slapped a Sister. I felt as though Sister Vera was dying to laugh but didn't quite dare over the book-throwing incident, and the Sister I slapped neither said nor did anything after I hit her. That confused me. I couldn't quite believe it. Nobody was acting the way they were supposed to.

I had been at the Home for over a year when Sister Gertrude said, "I can't understand you. This hard callous girl can't be you. What have I ever done to make you hate me so?" Maybe I wouldn't have cared even then, except that Sister Gertrude had tears in her eyes. Suddenly, I was ready to talk.

I begged, and I do mean begged Sister Gertrude to give me another chance. I felt terrible to see Sister cry. I wanted to tell her I loved her and was ashamed of the way I had been acting, and I really did say it. I begged Sister not to lose faith in me. Now that I am a mother, I feel as she must have felt on those days when I can't seem to handle my own children. Sister did reassure me, and she hugged me. From that day on I worked at making good. I talked often with Sister Gertrude. At times I would become very discouraged and depressed. Finally I told Sister I just felt mean and no good at times. I couldn't understand myself or why I did some things. So she gave me a piece of paper and a pencil and took me to a school-room. She said, "Now, Rosemary, you sit there and write down all the faults you think you have." Believe me, you never saw a list so long. She called me to her office and we hashed over the list. She crossed out quite a few things she didn't think were faults. Was I ever happy about that! Those left on the list we talked about. I tried to improve myself accordingly. As time went on I could see the difference myself. I began acquiring friends and succeeding on several levels. All of the Sisters were nice. I sat down and thought about that. I decided they must be liking me because I had changed. People in general were liking me for myself. What a wonderful feeling.

I got into everything: plays, the choral group, parties, ball games, tennis—everything. I also began getting interested in religion. I began by loving God a little, and pretty soon God was loving me a lot. Just the same, I figured it was going to take something pretty powerful to get me into heaven, so I began loving our Blessed Mother. That was something my own mother had taught me, but so many terrible things had happened in between that I had pretty well stopped praying.

Like always, however, I still lost my temper now and then.

Believe it or not, I began taking violin lessons. One day I was in the music room screeching out some notes when another girl came in with her two friends. She wanted to play the piano; I wanted to play the violin. What a racket that was. Finally, when the other girl couldn't stand my screeching any more, she rudely ordered me out of the room. No way. I was there first, and she had no business giving me orders. So I stayed. "If anybody goes," I told her, "it's *you.*"

"Get out," she yelled, "or I'll slap you silly."

"Heck, no!"

She slapped me a hard one. Was I surprised! But not too

surprised to stop me from throwing my violin at her. And I missed her, too.

The girl with me yelled, "Don't hit her back, Rosemary." I was so angry, furious in fact. What did I really want? To slug her, or walk away and keep my self-respect?

I walked away. To this day, I don't know how I managed.

Then I began thinking about my coming graduation. I had never dared dream that one day I would really and truly graduate from high school. But here it was, and each day the Big Day drew nearer.

With that came the thought that I would soon be taking my place in the world as a citizen, and depending on myself. That was a sobering thought. As June drew closer I began looking back over the past two years. Had so much really happened in so short a time?

I thought over my resentments, my angers, my hatreds. How they had seethed within me. Much of that seemed to be gone. I wished I'd paid more attention to all that I had learned, but it still was not too late. It had taken only time, trust, and a little growing up to accomplish all that I had done. I could apply all that I had learned to my everyday living.

Now I had to prepare myself for the world and its ways. And believe me, that way was going to be different.

TWELVE

Street Kids

JEAN'S stepfather began abusing her sexually when she was six years old. He initiated sexual relations with her on a regular once-a-month schedule when she was eight. Jean did not tell her stepmom because the two had never gotten along. "She was always accusing me of lying, and she would just have said that this was a bigger lie than ever."

The sexual abuse was physically painful, but Jean's stepdad told the child that he would buy her whatever she wanted in return and, she says, "he did." He also warned her that if she ever told he would have to go to jail, and all the goodies would end.

Jean wanted them ended, so she ran away when she was twelve.

She ran for several hundred miles.

Some adult street people took her in to the crude shelter they had constructed. They shared what little they had put together, and asked for nothing back. "They had couches and blankets," Jean says, "and I slept there and kept warm."

The pretty, clean, carefully dressed young woman has

lived, sort of, on the streets ever since. She has never prostituted and does not intend to. Her own mother sends her a little money, enough to get by on. She stays at the home of her current boyfriend and his sister, Jean's girlfriend.

Jean's early family life was complicated.

She lived with her real mother until she and her husband split up when Jean was two years old. Then Jean was placed in a foster home. Between the ages of two and six, she went through "at least twenty foster homes." (This is not as unusual as it sounds; I noted in the case history of one teenager placed in a Good Shepherd Home that she had been in twenty-six foster homes by the time she was fourteen.) Eventually, the foster parents with whom Jean lived from the age of six legally adopted her.

A child who has suffered through twenty foster-home placements by the time she is six years old, during the years when her needs for security and stability are most urgent, has by that very fact already been emotionally damaged.

Were the adoptive parents concerned when Jean ran away?

She shrugs. "People say my stepmom was worried; I don't know."

Have adult men given her trouble on the streets?

Well, yes. Attacked once by an older man, she escaped, although he did tear off her clothing. She fought him off. Once in a while Jean does drugs, "When I get so depressed."

Jean's primary relationships are with her street-brothers and street-sisters, many of whom also ran away from home because of sexual abuse. Jean attends an alternative school and sees a counselor there. Without that kind of help, this lovely young girl would already have become a prostitute or a dead body, or both.

A young boy she knows had run away from home because of

sexual abuse, and then found out that he could exist on the streets only by selling himself because he had nothing else to sell. He tried to hang himself but was found in time. He's in the hospital now.

Julie ran when she was eleven.

Her parents split up when she was eight and her sister was eleven; their baby brother was two. Julie's mother got custody but could not work because of the baby. The father, an attorney, did pay alimony but it seemed as though there was never enough money.

Once a month the two girls spent a weekend with their dad, and he also took them for a couple of weeks' vacation each year. With Dad the children could get whatever they wanted, and money seemed plentiful. He took them on trips. That's why they didn't say anything about the sexual relations he had with both of them. If they told, he warned them, he would go to jail and he could not take them for weekends, nor could he then pay anything to their mother.

Mother began seeing various boyfriends, and then one of them moved in. He also wanted sex with Julie.

"I couldn't take any more," says Julie; "I didn't try to tell my mom; I just left."

Julie was eleven years old.

Where has she lived?

"Everywhere. I come from California, but I've lived everywhere, from New York through the west coast.

"I went to the truckers first. That gave me a place to sleep at night and food. When I got a bit older, I became a prostitute. Had to."

Julie never had a pimp. "They take too much money," she

explains. "I couldn't afford that. I was taking care of two other street kids besides myself.

"I could prostitute because I was experienced; they weren't."

The pimps gave her a bad time, Julie states matter-of-factly. They beat her up several times. So she took karate, and became adept. She carries a weapon.

"Did your tricks always pay?" I asked.

"Yes. Some do try not to, but then I'd tell them I had a knife. They paid."

Julie quit school when she ran away and has never had a chance to attend again. She'd like to get her G.E.D. Eighteen now, she figures that she's done with prostitution. She hated it, but had no other way of surviving. Too young to get a job, she had no skills anyway.

When prostituting, Julie took drugs. "You have to do something to get you through it," she explains. Along the way she has worked at any kind of odd job she could pick up: waitress, receptionist, construction worker, plumber—helping out mostly.

Julie is tall and very, very thin. She considers herself fat and explains that she wore size one pants when living on the streets. She didn't always eat, and she didn't sleep every night. "I remember many nights when I didn't sleep at all," she says. "I walked all night long."

An alcoholic for a while ("I drank two fifths of Jack Daniels a day"), she leaves it alone now. Clearly very tired, Julie hopes that she can settle down someplace. She has found part-time work in a restaurant.

"I'm only eighteen," she said reflectively, "but I feel like I've lived for years and years."

"How much money can you make in one night?" I asked a fourteen-year-old girl.

"A thousand dollars." Her child's eyes were world-weary.

"That much?"

She shrugged. "It depends on your looks and how good you are. A trick might promise $100, but it's better than he expected. So he gives you $200. Easy."

She didn't look like it was easy.

I've stayed out on the streets myself, watching "the action."

I've seen a little girl clutching a doll hop in a car with a man, and the cars cruising for the young boys. Young boys are more in demand than young girls.

I've watched pimps driving around their territories, making certain that everyone is at work.

Across the country this year an estimated 150,000 children will run. To the bright lights and the cold streets.

I have hung around the bus terminals watching for the children. They are easy to recognize: a small backpack; looking bewildered, trying to appear grown-up; the girls with mascara and eyeliner, the boys with a bravado they do not feel.

I've watched the pimps' cars close by, big and beautiful cars. They would certainly impress a frightened runaway. I've watched the pimps talk to runaways, buy them food, get them into their cars. I've wondered why adult volunteers are not in the bus terminals, as interested in our children as are the pimps.

The age range of street kids is usually from thirteen to

twenty-two, although sometimes children as young as eight can be found there. Twice as many boys run as girls.

Almost three-quarters of the street kids are school dropouts or have been suspended from school.

Most teens who run away from home have been physically abused and often also sexually abused. Not every one of them, of course. We still know so little about them.

Most of the emotionally disturbed youngsters on the streets are likely to have been physically abused.

Juvenile offenders make up the third largest group on the streets. They are likely to be into drugs or alcohol, and to have been physically abused at home.

Street kids need food, employment, education, and mental-health counseling. Their next greatest needs are for shelter, clothing, vocational training, financial assistance, legal and medical services, dental care, foster care, and treatment for drug abuse.

The demands for services for them are staggering, particularly in the areas of individual counseling, drop-in centers, shelter, food, and health care.

Perhaps most street kids are children who would once have been placed in Good Shepherd or similar Homes. With the passage of legislation decriminalizing running away from home and extensive truancy from school, and the absence of adequate alternatives, only the streets are left for children to run to. So the youngsters who have been traumatized by abuse are not provided with the assistance they need and to which they are entitled. Unless they get help before adulthood, anything which might be done may come too late.

Julie, as I've said, no longer prostitutes.

"Did you ever enjoy it?" I asked.

"I hated it," she answered vehemently. "I hated it. I hated every bit of it.

"It was sick and mean and gross and nasty. I want nothing more to do with it. Not ever."

Julie survived until she became eighteen and could legally work. Many street kids don't survive: they commit suicide or they are preyed upon by adults or they starve or freeze to death.

The street kids are *our* children, *our* most valuable resource, *our* responsibility. Most of them are running from sexual and/or physical abuse. They tend not to talk about sexual abuse. They run.

Somehow we must help them tell their secret, break the silence, help them fight back.

THIRTEEN

Pearl

My HUSBAND and I have just celebrated our thirty-ninth wedding anniversary.

It's been a rough thirty-nine years.

I thought sex was something you did to make babies. I used to wish that God had provided an easier way.

I hated sex. I thought that was the only thing about me that my husband loved. I felt like a prostitute in my own marriage.

I was a high-school dropout, and married at seventeen.

Marriage was awful. I could give myself no reason for the loathing, and thought I must be crazy.

My childhood had been miserable too. The only time I can remember being happy was in church.

The days of my marriage dragged by. They were even worse than my childhood.

After two months, I ran away with a distant relative, a navy officer. Anything. It couldn't be worse than marriage. But I knew, deep down I knew, that he would leave me, and I would become a prostitute.

I could see the writing on the wall: prostitute.

So I went back to my husband and to hell.

He couldn't understand. He provided for me, we had a lovely home, I didn't have to work, he loved me.

He had grown up in a German community and thought a wife's place was in the home, taking care of the children and keeping everything safe for her husband. I kept saying, "But I want more."

What more?

I didn't know. There had to be more.

I thought I was crazy. Nothing else could account for my misery and depression. I had to be crazy.

Once my physician gave me tranquilizers. Perhaps those would help. But again I knew, deep down, that I wanted to swallow the whole bottleful and get peace. Final peace. Get everything still.

I stopped the tranquilizers. I didn't dare drink. I knew what I could do with drink. I was afraid of pills, all pills. I knew I could self-destruct.

We had six children. They were like two families. After the first three it was some years before the fourth, fifth, and sixth.

My sixth was a boy. I didn't like him, couldn't stand him. I was not a good mother. Sometimes I'd call a friend and ask her to take the child for a while. "I need a breathing space," I'd explain.

That kind of behavior was crazier than ever.

I decided to get into therapy.

I selected a counselor carefully, and I checked his credentials. He had a doctorate from Berkeley and a good reputation.

Either I saw him alone, with my husband, or with the whole family. Sometimes my husband saw him alone, as did some of my children, the three youngest.

I saw him for eight and a half years and was no better than when I started. If anything, I was worse.

My three children were into drugs.

Something, in fact, was terribly wrong with the children. Our marriage was on the verge of breaking up.

I changed therapists, and went to a woman therapist.

My real problem began to surface. But every time I tried to talk about it, my jaw went out of joint, and I couldn't talk at all.

My therapist was patient. By degrees I dared remember the incest which I had repressed, shut out of my conscious-ness all my life. The terrible, ravaging memories came back, one after the other. Even as a child and a teenager, I had not let myself know. I had locked each experience in a trunk and thrown away the key. It had been too awful to know, even in childhood.

As far as I can recall, my father molested me sexually from the time I was three until I was sixteen.

He never hurt me physically. He was a gentle, loving, kind, and generous man who had violated the depths of my being.

That repressed memory affected my whole life. It almost destroyed me.

My husband had been patient. We had both made a com-mittment to marriage, and we had stuck it out even though it had been hard. At last we could love and accept each other as we are. Then we turned our attention to our children.

What had gone wrong, we wondered. We talked with them; we listened.

Under the guise of therapy, my male counselor had sexually assaulted both of our sons and one of our daughters. The boys were eight and ten when they started with him, and our daughter was fifteen. Our daughter and one of the boys had been sexually used, body contact. One boy had been under continued, unrelenting pressure, but had resisted.

Our children said they had tried to tell us at the time, but we had not heard them.

My daughter had done what I did, repressed the whole thing. Her memory did not return until I asked her to write a letter describing the attacks. Then flashes returned. She was seeing a social worker at the time and he helped her remember.

After she had broken with my counselor, my daughter got into drugs—hard drugs. She had had one terrible auto accident while she was out cold with cocaine. She drank heavily, too.

One son got into pot when he was under heavy pressure from my counselor to become sexually involved with him. During his senior year in high school, he went to a treatment center and dried out. But he went back to drugs, also alcohol. He was then working with a priest-psychologist. The priest advised him to see a substance-abuse counselor. He joined AA and decided he was done with the whole thing. He's at the University now, studying mechanical engineering.

The other son got into pot, too, but was not deeply involved. He took a hard drug once but had such a bad trip that it frightened him. He has left hard drugs alone since. He is attending cooking school, hoping to become a chef.

We inquired into other families who had seen the same counselor, the one who'd assaulted our children. Several marriages had ended in divorce. The separation gave the counselor that much more control over the children so that he could the more easily induce them to get into sex with him.

My basic problem, incest, had never surfaced with him. He couldn't allow it to surface. If he had faced my personal problem of incest, he would have had to confront his own. Using children who were in a relationship of trust to him as a father figure was incest.

Three more families, whose children had been sexually abused by this same counselor, joined us in a lawsuit and we sued him. He can't practice any more, but he countersued.

Believe me, I know why people don't talk about sexual abuse. We ought to have been protected in some way so that he couldn't countersue. Two of the families don't have much money, and this is costing us a lot, but all four families are hanging in there. We hope to have all of this finished by the end of summer.

FOURTEEN

In the Business

DURING the 1830s, Bishop Benedict Joseph Flaget of Louisville, Kentucky, asked Sister Euphrasia Pelletier of Angers, France, to send a few of her Good Shepherd Sisters to the New World. He explained that out of a population of twenty-five to thirty thousand, Louisville had between 1,500 and 2,000 known prostitutes, women in need of redemption.

Sister Euphrasia had begun the Good Shepherd Congregation from the Sisters of Our Lady of the Refuge, a very small group of religious started by Father John Eudes in 1641 to operate refuges for those "fallen" women whom he had converted but who could not return home because they had been disowned by their families. Sister Euphrasia dispatched five Sisters to Louisville in 1842, only seven years after she had formed the Congregation destined to spread so quickly around the globe.

According to the annals of the Louisville Good Shepherd Order, the first prostitute knocked on the Sisters' door the first day they moved in and the second came the day after. The first asked for religious instruction, was baptized, and died in a few days. The second wanted only to be left alone. The Sisters prayed for her because she was seriously ill. Suddenly one night, she jumped up in bed and shouted, "I'm dying, get a priest." A young candidate for the Order went to the Louisville Cathedral and found a priest who came to tell the poor woman of God's mercy and love. She died later that night murmuring, "I believe, I believe."

When the Civil War broke out, the young men who had enthusiastically signed up brought along their wives and sweethearts, sure that the war would be over in a matter of days. But many were killed or moved forward, and the women were left behind. With no way of supporting themselves, they had to prostitute. One group of prostitutes operated four miles outside Columbus, Ohio. The City Fathers, worried for their children, went to the local clergy; after due consideration, the ministers said it would be better to leave the women where they were. Then the delegation went to a Catholic priest. "We will get the Sisters of the Good Shepherd," he said. The Sisters arrived in Columbus in 1865.

One seventeen-year-old who came to the Columbus Sisters had escaped from a house of prostitution and walked a long way to the Sisters' place, having heard about them from a ribald joke told by a trick the night before. She begged for admission. Two years earlier she had slipped away from the brothel and walked for miles to her own home in the rural area outside the city and knocked on the door—only to have it slammed shut in her face by her mother. She had no alternative but to return to the only way in which she could get a place to sleep and some food to eat. Now the Sisters welcomed her.

During those first days, they also welcomed a ten-year-old girl sent by the court because of lewd public dancing exhibitions set up by her mother. When she was allowed to leave the Sisters, the child refused to return home. In anger, the mother never saw her again, not even when the child was dying. She died young, the victim of child sexual abuse and neglect more than a century ago.

Last year, Sister Madonna of a Good Shepherd Home located in a southern city told me of a thirteen-year-old girl sent to the Sisters because of prostitution: she had already attained the status of her pimp's First Lady. ("First Lady" means that she presides over the stable, breaks in new candidates, travels with the pimp, and gets his sexual favors.) The child had run away from home because of sexual abuse there.

Good Shepherd Sister Kathleen recently told me about an exclusive call girl, sent to the Sisters instead of jail, who abandoned her trade for a successful marriage to a man "who was not one of my tricks, Sister." This young woman and her sister had gonorrhea by ages three and four, infected by one of their mother's boyfriends.

I had belonged to the Good Shepherd Sisters for only a few years when I first met a prostitute. Wanting to get off the streets but knowing no way of escape, she had phoned a county welfare service for help. The caseworker there had asked the Sisters at the Home in which I was then principal to take her. At that time we were not licensed to accept women over age eighteen, and Susie was twenty-two, but in light of her desperate need, we accepted her.

Because I had known almost nothing of the shady side of life before coming to the Good Shepherd, I was curious about Susie. For one thing, she was not especially good-looking and I had thought prostitutes must be alluring to attract men. And along with her came several trunkfuls of expensive clothing. Over the course of many months Susie became able to get rid of the fancy duds. She had brought exquisite jewelry, too, and found it more difficult to give that up.

Meanwhile, the men for whom she had worked were determined to get Susie back. They hung around the Home at night, calling out her name, and we had to request police protection. I could see for myself the difficulties inherent in a change of that life.

Over the years I have helped many a teenager who had been involved to some degree in prostitution in the manner I knew best: providing them with a good basic education and helping them attain vocational skills.

Not everybody made it. I especially remember a young woman who came knocking on the door of a western Good Shepherd Home, begging for immediate help. Her pimp had beaten her severely. Her face was black and blue and he had promised the woman that next time he would so disfigure her that she never could work again. She had come from a large Canadian city and wanted to get back there, but she knew that her pimp would have all the bus depots watched. One of the Sisters drove her to her home town; the girl was so frightened that she crouched on the car floor.

In a couple of weeks she was back in the U.S. And back with her pimp.

Getting out of prostitution is difficult. Generally the girl has been sexually abused at home, then has run away, never completed high school, and is without a marketable skill. Further, her pimp may have hooked her on drugs and alcohol; the craving drives her back into The Business again.

Edwina Gateley, a lay missionary, spends three nights a week from 9:00 P.M. until 2:00 A.M. hanging around street corners in Chicago talking to prostitutes. With the help of Chicago Catholic Charities, she obtained a building last year and made it the headquarters for her work with these women. According to Gateley, 94 percent of the prostitutes she has known were sexually abused in childhood.

Gateley tells one wonderful story. She told several of her prostitute friends that on a specific Sunday she would be giving a talk in church on the lay missionary movement. When she looked down on the congregation she was surprised to see, in the middle of that respectable group of church-goers, a pewful of her hookers dressed in their Sunday best and smiling up at her. They had come to give moral support to a friend.

In the play *The Best Little Whorehouse in Texas* the Madam extends her hand in greeting to the new candidate. "It was your father, I presume," she says.

According to a San Francisco study, interviews with street prostitutes, both male and female, indicated that the vast majority had been victims of incest, physical abuse, or rape prior to becoming prostitutes.

Sexual abuse at home, and economic circumstances, are generally the determining factors in the choice of prostitution. Attractive young women can also be pressured by parents or boyfriends or husbands into those kinds of sexual services which make money. When they become prematurely aged, or sick, or busted one time too often, these women are likely to be abandoned by those who have profited financially or taken advantage of their sexual services.

In 1977 over 50,000 people were arrested in the U.S. for prostitution.

In San Francisco in 1977, there were 2,938 arrests for prostitution. Of these 2,101 were of females for prostitution; 512 of males for prostitution; and 325 of customers of prostitutes. Among the prostitutes, many had been arrested several times.

In 1977, 414 people served time for prostitution in San Francisco; *not one* was a male customer.

Prostitutes are the most exploited of women.

Perhaps that explains Jesus's oft-repeated statement that prostitutes will make it into heaven ahead of folks like you and me.

In one large southwestern city the Good Shepherd Sisters operate a twelve-bed shelter for women in need: battered wives, drifters, women just out of messy divorces, prostitutes, and nonviolent offenders sent by courts. They have done this since 1977.

For years, Sister Carla has visited women in prison. Those who get to know her, and who are awaiting sentencing and would prefer to spend the time of their sentence with the Sisters, can ask Sister Carla whether the Sisters will accept them. For those women who appear willing to change their lives, and who will be sentenced for nonviolent crimes, the answer is yes.

The Sisters respect the women's privacy. There are three things the Sisters never ask women who come to the shelter, according to Sister Carla: "We never ask about their religion. We never ask for money. And we never ask what really was the problem that brought them here." Some of the cases accepted by the Sisters have become famous, much to the Sisters' dismay. Those stories in which women have really changed their lives seldom get told. The Sisters would say, "God's grace works most effectively in silence."

Bag ladies have come to this shelter; so have call girls and madams and ordinary prostitutes; so have young women ousted from their homes by stepmothers or by mothers who simply picked up and left.

During the first days after the shelter opened, a madam asked to come for her ninety-day prison sentence. Peggy had already been in The Business for fifteen years, and had only recently come to that city. When she opened a bordello in the area, the policeman on her beat sent word that she must pay him $600 a week, or else.

Peggy chose the or else. "If I had paid him only one dollar," she explains, "I would have been into organized crime. And that is a federal offense." Because she refused to pay, Peggy's Place was raided. She landed in jail, and there she met Sister Carla.

Peggy had been arrested before—several times, in several places. She had never been convicted before because, she thinks, she and her girls were always very discreet: they never, never gave out the names of the men who were their customers. No famous politician, no rich man, no respectable father of a family ever had to worry if he went to Peggy's Place.

Although Peggy had been in The Business a long time, it had not been her first choice for an occupation. But everything in life had set her up for prostitution. From the time she was seven years old her father beat her, viciously. Black eyes and a bruised body were her regular trademarks; she grew up expecting the worst. Her parents were only sixteen years older than she, and not prepared to cope with children.

Because of his violence, her mother divorced Peggy's father and married a second man who proved to be not much better than the first. Peggy was only fourteen when he first raped her. He assaulted her repeatedly. In fact, he got her mother drunk in bars and left her there to come home to bed with Peggy.

Peggy's mother did and didn't know. Mothers often (but not always) know when incest takes place, but deny this knowledge for a variety of reasons. For one thing, the daughter has become a threat to the mother; the mother, unconsciously at least, denies the incest so that she does not have to cope with her husband's infidelity. So it was with Peggy. When she finally did tell her mother, the mother threw her out and sent the sixteen-year-old girl packing.

"Incest leaves you feeling ashamed and guilty," remembers Peggy. "You feel that you are no good, damaged merchandise, and that you never can do anything good in life. You start out at the bottom of the heap."

By age twenty-two Peggy was already married to her second husband.

As we have seen, women who have been physically abused as children often select physically abusive mates. They have become so accustomed to abuse that, in some strange way, abuse is all they know, all they can feel at ease with. So it was with Peggy and her husband.

He was brutal. He beat Peggy regularly. Then at age twenty-six she had a baby. The infant needed surgery. Her husband had been telling his wife ever since he married her that she was sitting on a gold mine. Now he proceeded to demonstrate it.

He took her to one of his pals, a pimp, and said, in effect, "She's yours." To Peggy he said, "Don't leave until I come for you, or I'll kill you." Says Peggy, "I wanted to go out and get a gun and shoot him, but I was scared to. I'm scared yet that he'll find me."

Peggy was put to work on twelve-hour shifts: from 6:00 P.M. to 6:00 A.M. The money was good, even with the pimp taking 60 percent. Peggy saved the money for the baby's operation, looking forward to the day she would have enough.

In a few weeks her husband showed up and stole her money. They had one dreadful fight. He knocked her teeth out, broke several bones, and cut her with a knife, necessitating stitches in several places. Then he left, telling her that he was giving the baby up for adoption.

Just about everything had happened to Peggy by now: a physically abusive father, a sexually abusive stepfather, divorce, a physically abusive husband, forced prostitution—and a missing baby.

Many reasons have been put forward as the basic cause of women turning to prostitution. The bottom line only too frequently is the need for immediate cash. In Peggy's case, this was only too true: a husband who couldn't support his family; an infant in desperate need of medical assistance. And although Peggy had been an honor-roll student in high school, she had no skills to lean on that would bring in the immediate cash she needed. She had little choice but to support herself by prostitution.

But those few weeks as a hooker had been more than enough. Peggy would never prostitute herself again. Instead she recruited girls, often sexually abused at home like herself, and became a madam.

To get back to Peggy with the Good Shepherd Sisters at

their shelter, she had no sudden conversion. But the peaceful calm of the Sisters impressed her. Throughout the whole of her battered life, she had known very little about either peace or calm. She absorbed the quiet, and grew to love the peace.

Once released from the shelter, Peggy set up a respectable escort service: men could pay for escorts, but with the understanding that no sex was included. Peggy made that stipulation clear. Even so, the Sisters who had become her friends worried about the escort services.

Peggy was set up, she believes, for another arrest. Three men phoned for escorts in one evening; Peggy still has the telephone tape with her words on it: "Sex is not included."

Each of the men offered the girls extra money to get into bed with them, and each had a police officer in tow. The girls were arrested and so was Peggy. This time Peggy went to jail.

"That's when I decided to change my life, and when I got in touch, really and truly, with God," says Peggy. "I had not pondered long enough, or deeply enough, on my experience of living with the Sisters. It had been such a totally different experience for me that I had not been able to absorb it.

"When I was with the Sisters, I realized that prostitution is wrong. In prison, I began to suspect that God loves me, even me. Me, despite all the calamities of my life. I tried to let that love sink in, even as I doubted that *anybody* could really love me. Up until the Sisters, nobody ever had. My baby would have loved me, but I had lost even my baby.

"Prison is dreadful. Women prisoners, like prostitutes, are primarily victims. We all lived from day to day. We made one day at a time, and we made our peace with God, and begged him to let us die before we got out again into the coldness and cruelty of life."

Peggy has continued her close friendship with the Good

Shepherd Sisters. She has gone into the printing business and hopes, eventually, to own and manage her own shop. And she has found her daughter.

Eighteen years old now, the daughter had hunted for her mother, aching for her mother's love as much as that mother longed for her. Through their mutual efforts, they found each other.

Peggy has not forgotten her "girls" either. "They're caught," she explains, "in a web of difficult circumstances. They cannot support a child or children, and their walked-out husbands are certainly not contributing to child support. Welfare gives women something like $75 a child a month; one cannot even engage a sitter for that much. If a john offers a woman $200 for an evening spent with him, it's tough to refuse, even though, with the many sexual diseases now in circulation, she stands a chance of becoming infected."

Remarkably free from bitterness, Peggy never complains that life has dealt her a rough hand to play—although she could, with reason. She remarks only on the unfairness of arresting prostitutes but not the men who solicit and pay them.

Besides, Peggy is in love, really in love for the first time in her whole life. She chats merrily away about her prospective husband for minutes at a time, shifting only to discuss her daughter and tell about the latest in mother-daughter disputes as to exactly when that daughter should be in at night.

With the continued support and friendship of the Sisters, Peggy has made it. The obstacles to her success in life were monstrous. Peggy has overcome them all, and done so with a smile and a charm which enhance the inner beauty of a woman who, having been victimized, has triumphed.

Peggy's story points out, I think, the futility of arresting prostitutes, or raids and jail sentences. The choice made by these young women has generally been determined for them by the brutalizing effects of early life experiences. Until those experiences have been shorn of their degrading power, a female prostitute is unlikely to change her mode of employment.

Peggy is just over forty years old. Until I questioned her about her early sex abuse, she had never been asked. Neither had any law enforcement agency bothered to inquire into her early years of brutal physical battering. And of course she hadn't volunteered the information.

The Good Shepherd Sisters whom Peggy knew had followed the course which I would have chosen had I worked with Peggy at the shelter. They don't ask questions; the Sisters are simply present, lovingly present, and available for whatever counseling their residents might seek. They offer the only kind of treatment which I know to be effective: openness and time to listen, along with a caring love.

Who is the greater offender: the prostitute who was forced to discover as a child that sex is for sale, or you and I who pass judgement on prostitutes?

How many and what variety of men, unknown and unseen by polite society, seek out prostitutes?

How many women, now respectably married or in eminent positions in this modern world, have once been prostitutes?

And in that shelter, who ministers to whom: the Sister to the prostitute, or the prostitute to the Sister?

In meeting Peggy, I was introduced to a person with a much greater degree of courage, perhaps, than I had ever before encountered. I met a woman who is intellectually gifted, cheerful, loyal, and devoid of bitterness or self-pity. I could not do other than recognize the dignity and the wholeness which she has struggled to maintain despite the severity of her victimization. My friendship with Peggy, as well as with the many women who have been caught up in prostitution, is respectful. Why Jesus should have preferred to eat his dinner with "those people" rather than with the dignitaries who run our systems in business, economics, politics, and churches is clear to me.

If only you and I could sit down and chat with women of the streets and share in a thoughtful interchange and gradual self-revelation, we might discover that we share more than we imagine.

We can look at the prostitute and think, "There but for the grace of God go I." But those words could also be echoed by the prostitute who, aware of our hypocrisy and pride and self-caring, could say them when she looks at you and me.

Unfortunately the ministry to street women—drifters, prostitutes, bag ladies, and prisoners—is looked upon as a marginal ministry in the churches. Mainstream efforts are directed primarily to the middle and upper classes. But, in fact, ministry to those on the fringes of society *is* the specific ministry of the churches, which were founded to speak the good news to the poor.

So what is the answer?

I wish I knew, but I don't.

This, however, I do know: the arrest and imprisonment of prostitutes and the criminalization of prostitution is not only wrong; it misses the point.

FIFTEEN

Jenny and Patsy

JENNY'S seven-year-old brother began sexually abusing her when she was six years old, doing such things as slipping into her bed at any hour during the night. She told her mother, who ordered the boy to stop, but he didn't. Jenny's father also asked the boy to keep out of his sister's room, but still he would not.

When Jenny was sixteen she moved out and found an apartment. She had attended school regularly but dropped out as she was going into the twelfth grade.

Hanging around with other girls who prostituted, Jenny began prostituting herself; she needed money to live on and had no other way of getting it. This life continued for up to three years. The money was not the greatest, she says, but it was enough.

Jenny did not get pregnant as a prostitute, but since quitting she has had two children. Both pregnancies resulted from love affairs. Because she needed help to get through pregnancy she went to Birthright, a nondenominational network organized to assist pregnant women in whatever ways they might need. There Jenny met Good Shepherd Sister Renee. "She helped me through a lot of it," says Jenny. "I talk a lot to Sister Renee. We've worked through the whole sex-abuse thing too. She's a very nice person, a sweet lady."

Jenny gave up her children for adoption. Although she knows where they are, she doesn't ever see them because the children would not recognize her as their mother. But it's a comfort to her to know that both children are in good homes and well cared for.

Right now, Jenny has physical problems and is not working, but she will go back to work soon, she thinks. She does babysitting occasionally and does enjoy that.

Since she was sixteen Jenny has been on her own. Life has not been easy, but she is making it.

My name is Patsy.

I was five years old when my uncle, who was babysitting for me and my seven-year-old sister, began abusing me sexually. I told my parents; they listened, they believed me, and they did nothing about it. The abuse and the babysitting kept going on.

It made me feel bad and hurt, depressed and angry. I cried often, and for long periods of time, but nobody cared.

I discovered why nobody did anything about my uncle when my mother, father, brother, and a second uncle also began sexually abusing me. Sexual abuse was our family's secret, handed down from generation to generation.

In spite of my misery, or perhaps because of it, I went to school regularly. School was a place to get away to, although concentrating on schoolwork was difficult.

I didn't like to be sexually used. I hated it. I wanted to escape from it. Finally, when I was thirteen, I ran away.

Because I was determined not to get caught I ran far away, out of state. I lived in two different states, and stayed with elderly people, and worked on farms for my food. I never gave anybody my real name, and I always said I was older than I was.

But everything got to be too much. I went to the police and turned myself in. I explained why I had run away, and they believed me. After that, I spent a whole year in a psychiatric hospital. From there I went to a residential treatment center for girls, and there I met Sister Renee.

At the center I met a lot of sexually abused teenagers, and we had sexuality groups. We talked about our feelings and struggles and pain, with a counselor to help us. I stayed there for four years, and I needed every speck of that time.

I got to know Sister Renee, and talked to her a lot. My family is Catholic and I had been baptized, so Sister prepared me for First Communion. I love Sister, and I still meet with her.

After leaving the treatment center I dated a young man and got pregnant. Then he invited his friends in, and they had sex with me, too. I caught on to his tricks: those men were paying him. He had turned me into a prostitute.

One day I refused to go down to the job he had set me up in. We argued, and he shot me in the leg. He had fought in the Vietnamese War and using a pistol came naturally to him. After he shot me he sold the pistol to some other guy so it could not be traced.

I pressed charges but the case was dismissed because he told the court that he didn't speak English, which was a lie. He knew English only too well.

One of the boys I had known in grade school then came back into my life and we got married. My baby is beautiful.

I had gotten to know old people when I ran away, so I turned my house into a daycare for elderly people whose relatives couldn't take care of them during the day. I made a couple of hundred dollars a week that way. My husband runs his own business.

We are going to have our own child fairly soon, so I'm not working now. We're looking forward to the baby and, later on, I'll go back to daycare for the elderly.

I did graduate from high school after I left the residential care, and I'm proud of that.

My husband and baby and I go to church on Sundays and try to make a good life for ourselves. I came through the sexual abuse and survived it. I've left it behind me. It's not *my* problem any more; it's the problem of those who did it to me.

My mother and brother went to counseling also, with counselors at the treatment center. They got the help they need.

Whenever I want to, I can go back to the counselors and talk to them. That helps because sometimes I feel depressed.

But as for sexual abuse, it's over. It ended with me. It's not going to be passed on. We make our own lives. Other people can come through it and survive too.

SIXTEEN

In Prison

ACCORDING to Carolina Torrez, developer and director of a Christian halfway house for women released from prison, about 95 percent of all women in prison have been sexually abused, most of them by relatives at home, "someone they loved and trusted."

Carolina is on the Board of Catholic Charities, and a member of the Archbishop's Women's Commission, both in Seattle, and is on the National Board of Clergy and Laity Concerned, founded to bring issues of peace and justice to the attention of politicians and the President. A former newspaper editor, Carolina has conducted extensive research into all aspects of women's correctional centers.

Carolina's estimate that 95 percent of women in prison have been sexually abused agrees with the experience of Sister Thelma: many women in prison, Sister Thelma told me, have been sexually abused. According to research done by the National Coalition of American Nuns, "over 90 percent of the women in prison today were victims of incest attacks in childhood."

Understanding that incest demeans a person, robs her of self-respect, and leaves her feeling devalued, we can understand some of the reasons behind those offenses which result in imprisonment for women.

A study of the crimes for which women are sentenced reveals additional reasons.

Even when they commit the same kind of crime, says Carolina, women are often sentenced more severely than their male counterparts. For example, a sixteen-year-old girl and her boyfriend banded together to rob a store. While the young man held up the convenience store, the girl went off to find some drugs. In the course of a scuffle the boyfriend shot and killed a customer. The teenage girl was nowhere near the scene of the killing at that time. The fact was known and agreed upon in court. The girl got life, and the man was given a lesser sentence.

Says Carolina, "The judge, asked the reason for the discrepancy, answered: 'I did it for her own good, and because she was pregnant.' Apparently being pregnant made the crime that much worse."

This particular teenager had never before been in trouble with the law, had not even truanted from school.

I once met a young woman who, as a teenager, had been given two consecutive life sentences by a judge. She had been sitting in the car while her boyfriend robbed a store and killed a man in his way. The girl had been no way involved, and had done nothing to assist in the robbery or shooting. In court, however, she acted like a giddy teenager and told the judge that regardless of the sentence he gave, she could do it standing on her head. So he handed out two consecutive life sentences.

For some strange reason not understood by women, says

Carolina, in Washington State a prisoner who is giving birth is shackled to the delivery table. "Clearly," said Carolina, "some man made up that rule. Only a man could have supposed that a woman in labor could jump up off the table and escape out of the hospital." Nevertheless, that rule is adhered to.

Moreover, the newborn baby is immediately whisked away, and the mother in prison and her child have no opportunity of bonding. She does not see the child again until she leaves prison. In Washington State Carolina found that over 80 percent of women in prison are mothers whose children are separated from them.

One might ask, "If mother-child relationships are so important, why did the mother commit a crime?"

Most women in prison are there for economic nonviolent crimes, says Carolina. They steal or sell themselves to feed their children. They get caught, are locked up, feel themselves that much more demeaned, are not given preparation for good jobs when they leave, and are again forced to steal or prostitute. The cycle endlessly repeats itself as the woman lives out the victimhood for which incest had prepared her.

Women in prison are subjected to sexual invitations from male guards. Carolina described the degradation of one woman—"she is beautiful," says Carolina—who when undressing, hears male guards up on the catwalk calling out such taunts as, "You look great, baby."

Carolina says that she has compiled figures which demonstrate that it costs the state between $50,000 and $70,000 to feed and clothe one woman in prison for a year. She can set up a halfway house as an alternative to prison which would cost $5000 a year per woman, and in that halfway house provide counseling to help women socially and emotionally, and offer them adequate education for worthwhile employment.

The entire legal system, Carolina told me, is insensitive to the needs of women: lawyers, judges, prosecutors, administrators of the penal system. For example, all men's prisons have extensive law libraries; women's do not. Educational opportunities for women are usually inferior to these for men: in Washington State, notes Carolina, women can qualify for their G.E.D. and can prepare themselves for only low-paying jobs; men can qualify for educational-release time, and go out to college.

Those problems which route women to prison usually begin with sexual abuse. We see over and over again that incest victims do not usually complete high school because they run away from home as soon as they can take any care of themselves. Robbed of self-respect they lack the motivation to climb upward on the economic ladder. Their marriages often fail because, unconsciously, they tend to select abusers as husbands. They end up with children to support and feed.

They prostitute or steal. On and on it goes.

Can anything be done?

The answer is yes. Alternatives to prison can be developed which enable women to develop self-esteem, learn social skills, get a good education, and benefit from counseling.

The best time to remedy the situation is, of course, when the abuse occurs. At that time each member of the entire family needs individual therapy, joint family counseling, self-help and support groups.

Unless the victim speaks out about incest when and as it happens, these supports cannot be offered. As always, speaking out equals fighting back.

SEVENTEEN

Lynn

SISTER Harriet, who works with prisoners in a variety of situations, told me about Lynn.

Would I like to meet her? Sister Harriet asked. Lynn had been severely abused, she said, had killed her own child, and was serving a life sentence.

As would most people, I had little sympathy for a woman who killed her own child, regardless of the circumstances. But Sister Harriet had already set up the appointment, and reluctant to disrupt her plans, I agreed to meet Lynn.

Lynn, it turned out, was attending college on a study-release program. As we drove to the college, I found myself even more out of sympathy with a woman who would use a life sentence for killing her child as an opportunity to attend college. I was uncomfortable about meeting her.

Carefully dressed and groomed, Lynn was soft-spoken and courteous. In the car, on the way to the restaurant at which we planned to have lunch, I explained to Lynn that the sexually abused person is my primary interest at this time.

"My second husband sexually abused me," she said, "and during my childhood my mother physically abused me." The young woman's eyes filled with tears.

"And what was that like?" I asked.

Lynn's mother had six children. She beat each of them, but Lynn most of all. She tied the children to bannisters, or beds, or whatever was convenient. She said that God told her to do that. She locked Lynn in closets. God told her to do that, too.

At one point her mother told Lynn that God had ordained that Lynn follow in her mother's footsteps and take over the heavy work she was doing for God. One child was retarded; the mother said a witch had cast a curse on him and God had told her to beat the witch out, to do reverse witchcraft to get rid of the witch. God told the mother that the witch was hiding out in Lynn and Lynn was the person to beat. She held two of Lynn's fingers on a red-hot stove to burn the witch out; she burned off the tips of Lynn's fingers to below her finger nails, but the witch held on; the boy was still retarded.

Sick with pain, Lynn went to her minister. "Does God really talk to her?" she asked. "Your mother is trying to be a Christian, and she is a good tithe-paying church member," said the minister. "It would seem that she is trying to please God, and she believes that he told her to act as she has done. Whether or not he really did, I can't say."

Lynn's mother often kept her out of school; even in kindergarten she was kept out for six months. She made it to the seventh grade, she thinks, because her dad sent her to her aunt's house to live.

There Lynn got the only love and guidance she had ever received during her formative years. She began to feel that she was a person. But the placement didn't last, because the mother wanted Lynn back. She quit school to work and help support the family.

Lynn was married at seventeen, and the couple lived in a northern city for four years. The marriage was a good one, and Lynn had two children. In the meantime, the mother had made a couple of suicide attempts, and the neighbors phoned Lynn to say that her mother needed her and she ought to come home. So Lynn and her family moved next door to her mother.

Lynn's husband got a slight case of TB and had to go to the hospital. The mother visited him faithfully, brought fruit to him, and told him that Lynn was a whore, and that she had been a whore since she was twelve years old. Because the mother went on at great length and succinctly described the men whom Lynn brought home, the husband believed her. At that time Lynn was pregnant with her third child. Still struggling for her mother's love, Lynn asked her mother, with her husband present, why she had beaten her so much as a child. Enraged, the husband picked up his whore of a wife, and threw her out of the door. She had a miscarriage and began hemorrhaging. The mother took her home and prayed over her for two days, while Lynn continued bleeding. The mother would not call a doctor because she did not believe in doctors.

When the mother left the house for a short time, Lynn crawled on her hands and knees to their next-door neighbor and begged her to call an ambulance. "I got to the hospital," she remembers, "just in time."

The mother finally OD'd, and Lynn's marriage ended. Lynn's mother had succeeded in brainwashing the young husband to believe the accusations she hurled at Lynn.

Two years later, Lynn married again. Her husband had a prison record for rape, robbery, and drugs. "But I believed I was so evil that I should be grateful to anybody who said 'I love you,' and especially anybody who would ask me to marry him. I believed my mother. I believed that I had caused my brother's retardation. I couldn't remember ever being a whore, ever having a relationship with anybody except my first husband, but my mother said I was. Even a convict was too good for me."

The second husband's mother came to the small family, and asked for $100 a week. Lynn was holding down two jobs to support her children and to keep her husband in liquor and drugs; he didn't work. They couldn't possibly give the mother $100 a week, but she said they owed it to her as repayment for the bail she had shelled out for her son. So they added on that obligation.

Lynn had two children; the second, a boy, was retarded. The evil influence of Witch Lynn again. Lynn felt more guilty, more unworthy, more ashamed to be alive.

Her husband beat her, of course. She had lived with beatings all her life, and was almost accustomed to them. He also stole money from her. Anyhow, says Lynn, "I gave it to him. I wanted him to be happy so he would hold me in his arms and say 'I love you.' Never mind that he beat me thirty minutes later.

"He abused me sexually, too. I really think he was a homosexual, or maybe bisexual. He raped me violently, many times. Sexually, nothing was normal. The abnormal sex degraded me much more than all the beatings. I felt like an animal.

"And he beat the children. That's what worried me. He was at home all day with them. But he did accept my retarded son, although, like my mother had said, he believed he was possessed. I believed that, and believed he was possessed because of me.

"I came home from work one day and found marks all over my little boy's body. My husband was going to school at the time. He said that his mother did it. My mother had told me that I was going to pay for all the evil I did, so I thought that the mistreatment of my children was some kind of paying for all my sins.

"The next day I went to work. The child had a seizure, and my husband phoned me. I came home. We took the child to the hospital. The doctor noticed the bruises all over him, and asked what happened. I had no explanation. The baby was taken away from me. But I loved him, and wanted him with me. I paid two lawyers to get him back.

"We were living in the north, but I decided to move to the south, and invest in my sister's business. Actually, I was just trying to run away from my problems, but the problem was my husband, and I brought him along. We lived in small rural places. I knew the child abuse was going on. Sometimes I'd take my three children—I had had a daughter by my second husband—and put them in the station wagon, lock the doors, and drive away for a few hours of peace for them and me. I gave him all the money I made so he could get his drugs and liquor—anything to keep him happy.

"I should have left him. But I did so want somebody to hold me in his arms and say, 'I love you,' and make all my decisions for me. I'm so ashamed; it was all my fault, my selfishness. I asked the visiting nurse to come and teach me how to deal with a retarded child, but my husband would not let her in the house.

"One evening, he punched my retarded child in the

stomach with his fist, hard. I was sitting in a corner. I couldn't do anything; he would beat me too. I should have left him, I knew I should have left. But I was scared, and I had no place to go.

"When I was in the house, I kept Billy with me, because every day when I came home he had a different bruise. The night after the blow to his stomach the child had a seizure. I grabbed him. He seemed to be choking. I put my hand in his throat and bits of food and blood came out. I had no phone. My sister came, and I begged her to run to our nearest neighbors and get help. I screamed for a doctor. My baby took his last breath while my sister was there.

"The police came and noted the bruises on my child's face and body. The next day they arrested me. They wouldn't even let me go to his funeral. They said I was too dangerous.

"My husband wouldn't tell me where he was buried. At the preliminary hearing, both my husband and I were arraigned. Two attorneys were there, so I assumed one represented each of us. They didn't. They both represented my husband. He got off on bail. I didn't.

"Later, my bail was paid. The case was pending for two years. Meanwhile, I had another baby. My husband came to the hospital and started a fight, and he was going to take my baby away from me. It was stormy and raining outside. I wrapped the baby up and walked out of the hospital two days before I should have. I thought that the baby would take care of things, and my husband would really love me.

One night he picked up the baby and started to leave. I turned to the phone, called the police, picked up a knife, and stabbed my husband. The police never came, they don't bother about domestic fights. My husband went to the hospital and came back stitched up. He was enraged. He went to are police and told them a story. In the end, my baby died of SIDS. Then I found out where my husband had buried my retarded son; in a pauper's grave, separated from his biological daughter. Even in death, my child had been in his way.

"All my fault. I wondered how my children could love me. My baby had cried and pleaded when I came home from work, and I had not listened. I should have left and taken the children. But I needed so much to have somebody put his arms around me and say, 'I love you.' He didn't love me, of course, because I was too evil for love. Too unworthy. Too low.

"When I went to school to meet with my children's teachers, I noticed people backing away from me. I thought it was because I was so evil. I never dreamed that my husband was spreading the word that I killed my child.

"When my case came to trial, he was picked up as a devoted husband and father who had failed to adequately protect his children from me. While we were both in prison he told me, 'Lynn, I still love you. If you will write to the judge and say that I was not responsible in any way, I'll take care of the children while you are in prison.'

"I wrote the letter. I never breathed a word about him at the trial. I took all the guilt. I was offered a chance to plea-bargain, but I couldn't do that, because then I would have to say that I killed my child, and I didn't. I could have gotten a much-reduced sentence if I had plea-bargained, but I couldn't lie about abusing my children. So I got life.

"I will never tell the judge about my husband. My husband knows how much I love the children. If I tell, he'll harm them. I can't talk, not ever.

"My children are now in foster homes. We love each other, and I see them about once a month.

"Sister Harriet has helped very much. She has given me some sense that I am not bad. That I never was a witch. That my retarded brother and my baby never were possessed. That I did not deserve to be beaten. That I never was a whore. That I can learn. That people might love me. That my mother never heard God talking directly to her. That God did not do all this to punish me.

"The prison superintendent has been very kind, too. I couldn't figure out why she and Sister Harriet were so good to me. At first, I wondered what they were trying to get out of me. I was suspicious for many months. I didn't dream anybody could like me, want to help me, or get interested in my welfare.

"Sister Harriet found a person to tutor me, and I passed my G.E.D. Now I'm going to college. I never thought I could. I never even dreamed of getting an education. I never thought I was good enough.

"Now, at thirty-six, I'm just learning how to feel, how to act around people. I used to feel that everybody was out to get me. In prison I set myself up, at first, for solitary so I could get away from people. They all hated me, I thought.

"When I came to prison, I was more frightened by kindness than by punishment. I was used to beatings, but I had hardly ever experienced love.

"Sister Harriet persuaded me to go to college. Even yet, I guess, I'm trying to figure out why she's concerned about me. *"Me!"*

Listening to this lovely woman, I kept thinking of the compulsive and repeated sadism of her mother. The mother had physically abused all the children, but she hurt and persecuted Lynn throughout her entire life.

Prison is dreadful. But for Lynn, in her circumstances, prison was almost a gift: no more beatings, a chance for some education, an opportunity for kind treatment.

Finally, in prison she met Sister Harriet; Sister opened up horizons of which Lynn had never dreamed.

EIGHTEEN

Raising Children Who Tell

PSYCHOANALYST Alice Miller writes that all of us have been raised since childhood to believe that anything shameful which happens to us must be our fault. Somehow we, the victims, are to blame. This notion has helped conceal the child sexual abuse which we now know cuts through all levels of society, economics, race, and religion. That attitude must be changed.

Somehow we must learn to raise children who tell.

That means we are called upon to raise children who are self-confident, independent, socially adept, and informed—yet do this without allowing the pendulum to swing to the other extreme of cultivating child tyrants.

The development of a climate of openness in the home is urgent. Children need to feel that they can bring any story, and problem, to the attention of either parent and they need to know that the parent will take time for them.

Can this be done with both parents at work? It can. I know and often visit a family in which both parents are executives. The parents are busy, stressed, and often harassed. When I visit, I usually stay for dinner. Regardless of what unfinished business hangs in the balance, both parents give their children total time and attention during the dinner hour and for at least an hour after dinner. I began dropping in about six years ago, when the daughter was seven and the son was nine. Even without our friendship I would have continued visiting, just to enjoy the parents' ongoing relationship with their children, and the open, tension-free atmosphere in which the children are growing up. Within the small family circle, whether or not both parents work, this atmosphere *can* be developed.

Some families stress to children that nothing in the family is to be discussed outside of the family. This kind of enforced secrecy is dangerous for the child. Under any circumstances it's difficult for a child to tell people in authority about a relationship with an adult which feels wrong; if that adult is a relative, and if the parents are obviously bent on maintaining a facade of respectability at any cost, the child's fears of telling become even more aggravated.

Children need help in developing good, wholesome self-images. Their small successes should be noted and praised. They need guidance in dressing appropriately, and in everyday courtesy, so that other adults will praise them. Children ought to be given special tasks around the home in which they can achieve tangible results.

Children growing up in homes with strict discipline, anger, and physical abuse are at greater risk of sexual abuse because they become fearful of telling parents anything.

The rural area in which I spent my childhood must have been one of the most innocent oases in the world: all immigrant farmers working from dawn to dusk seven days a week; no crime; no police; no locked doors; no theft. Boys scribbling on windows with wax candles during Halloween is the worst offense I can recall.

But even into that paradise came a child molester.

I was seven years old and playing near construction workers who were adding a second room to our rural one-room school. One builder, older than my father, seemed especially nice, so I often stopped to wish him good morning as I ran out to play; my home was close to the school.

One day he took me on his lap, and began a tickling game. I laughed but sensed something wrong because of where he was tickling me, even through my clothing. I told my mother about it, not being sure whether it was wrong or right.

"I'm sure he didn't mean any harm," she said calmly, "but he shouldn't have done that. I'll tell Daddy, and he'll talk to the man. You can say 'Good morning' to him, but don't let him touch you again."

She had handled the situation superbly. She displayed no anger or undue fear, she made it clear that I was not to blame, and she let me know that a strong figure, my father, was taking care of me.

Because of the very young age at which children are likely to be abused, a child should know before starting school which areas of the body are private and not to be touched: those areas covered by a bathing suit. And children should be helped to differentiate between good and bad touching. Within the family, children can be given a warm hug and kiss; teachers and bus drivers and strangers should not give such caresses. And the child should be able to say, "I don't like that. Stop it." Or, "I don't want to kiss you." Or, "I'm going to tell my mother."

A child who is able to say these kinds of words to a relative such as a grandparent, or a teacher, is a youngster who will say "No" in the family home, at times and in situations when parents expect obedience. The child's negative response should be graciously accepted, and the child taught to express it appropriately.

Children should not be taught obedience to all adults. Neither should children be expected to obey parents without question at all times. The child's independence should be respected and nourished; the child is a person and should be considered one. If the child does not want to kiss Aunt Annie, then Aunt Annie should graciously go without the kiss.

The child who comes to a parent with a story of any kind of sexual abuse should be listened to. In general, children are unlikely to make up such stories—although, a word of caution, that has happened. If the matter seems doubtful, then the child should be taken to a diagnostic center for testing and evaluation before accusations are made.

A male who accuses Granddad or Uncle Johnnie should not be dismissed with, "Oh, Granddad was just playing with you, he doesn't mean any harm," or "Your Uncle Johnnie loves you, that's all." Neither should the panic button be pushed. Rather, Granddad and Uncle might be observed in their relationship with the child, or the child's father might have a talk with Granddad just as my father did with the construction worker.

At the same time, it should not be forgotten that 10 percent of child sexual abuse within the family is done by Granddad; and usually, he had abused the child's mother when she was growing up. According to Steven Wolf of Northwest Treatment Associates, a father might, given treatment, stop abusing his own children, but then begin again after he becomes a grandfather.

Children who develop vaginal or rectal irritations may have been assaulted. Children with such problems should be taken to a pediatrician for an examination which includes tests for venereal diseases. Alarming numbers of children are suffering from gonorrhea, syphilis, or herpes.

If a child has VD, all family members should be examined.

Parents need to deal gently with children who develop apparent phobias about school, preschool, or daycare. The tearful pleading to stay home may indicate a simple problem which can easily be handled, or it may be connected to sexual abuse at the school or day-care facility. Parents need not become obsessed with fears about child sexual abuse, but they could become more watchful than is currently the case.

Parents wanting to instill respect in their children for certain professionals, such as ministers or policemen or teachers, need to avoid stressing respect for *all* ministers or *all* policemen or *all* teachers. Abusers can be found in any occupation, and the more respectable, the better the cover.

In my own family home, priests were regarded with great respect. My parents loved nothing better than inviting a priest to dinner, and quoting his wisdom. I picked up the message: you can always trust a priest; a priest will do no wrong.

I had entered the convent at seventeen, and I had had no personal experience with sex or sexual encounters.

I was in my twenties when I noticed a priest who was conducting a retreat for us Sisters looking at me in a way which made me very uncomfortable. When the last day came, I thanked God he was leaving. He couldn't go too soon.

The superior met me. "Run up to Father's room and help

him with his luggage," she asked.

I was speechless. I opened my mouth, and then closed it. I had no proof. If I said, "I don't like the way he looks at me," she would probably have leaped to his defense. With my heart in my mouth, I went upstairs.

His eyes said that he was utterly delighted to see me.

Would I fasten his collar, he asked; he had trouble reaching it. Standing as far away from him as possible I fastened it, knowing the request was totally inappropriate.

Then he handed me his suitcase.

I tried to fling it into the elevator with the intention of running down the stairs, but he was standing behind me. Reluctantly, I got in, and hit the button. It was one floor down and the elevator door closed automatically. Immediately he had me in his arms for a kiss which was not a fatherly kiss. "I only want to say goodbye," he said. The door opened and I fled.

He returned occasionally to visit the entire community. When he did, either I was not in the same room with him, or I kept my eyes down someplace beneath the carpet. I tried to be as unassuming and invisible as possible. But my avoiding him was noticed. "You lead men on," my superior said, "and then have to take special precautions. He's a fine priest. I don't want one word spoken about him." She had said only what I had expected anybody to say about a priest; naturally, everybody would assume it was my fault, all my fault.

Never mind that I had never spoken a word to the man.

In fact, I have never spoken a word to anybody about him from that day to this, because I knew I would be blamed.

The atmosphere of respect for priests in which I had been raised had intimidated me; any other man who asked me to fasten his collar would have been told how to do it in three short words.

There is one sensitive and final issue to deal with: the trial, and the child or adolescent as witness.

When a youngster does manage to "tell on Dad," at his trial she is likely to retract her statements for the sake of her family. With incest, the entire family is disrupted: the relative brought to trial, and the child removed from the home. The victim feels that everybody's suffering is "all her fault," and other members of her family may have already told her so.

Usually, the sexual abuse has gone on in the home for some years before it is exposed. The youngster may have accepted it until adolescence, when he or she felt capable of making and sustaining independent decisions. A teenager may run from home and, if picked up, then reveal the abuse.

If the case is going to go before a grand jury or be prosecuted in court, the youngster needs preparation for the experience. Only last week I heard of a case in which a boy was summoned to court to testify against his father for sexual abuse; from his seat in court, the boy literally *crawled* on his hands and knees to the witness box so that he wouldn't have to see his father. Then he sat down and looked straight into Dad's eyes. He refused to testify.

The boy's caseworker, or an attorney, should have minutely described the entire court procedure to him before the trial; brought the youngster into the courtroom to be acquainted with the physical set-up; prepared him to face the relative in question; and provided extensive emotional support. If these safeguards couldn't be provided, and if the victim was the only available witness, the case should not have been brought to trial.

One more atrocity I might mention: in California, some

months ago, a judge sent a child into solitary confinement in jail for refusing to testify against her stepfather. (The man had been reported for sexual abuse after having voluntarily asked for therapy.) What psychological distress that action compounded in the child who was already a victim, I don't want to know.

In '82 a judge in Wisconsin sentenced a man who had sexually assaulted a five-year-old girl to ninety days in a work-release program. He explained the leniency with these words: "I am satisfied we have an unusually sexually promiscuous young lady. And he (the defendant) did not know enough to refuse. No way do I believe he initiated sexual contact."

Enough said. Why children hesitate to tell about sexual abuse should be clear.

NINETEEN

Moving On

As I reach the ends of several stories—of Rosemary's, Marcie's, Angela's, Iris's, and Pearl's—I find some mention in each as to the help each woman states she derived from her religious faith. Before going on, I need to explain my own position.

What my own life would have been like without religion, without a firm belief in a loving God, I cannot even imagine. Because of the paramount role the Catholic Church and the Good Shepherd Sisters have played in my life, it's only natural that most of my experiences have revolved around it. In the same way, it's very common for others, even strangers, to want to talk to me about God, about faith, about religion.

The same would be true, I think, no matter what my life's work had been. If I had been an artist, people would want to talk with me about art. If I had been a physician, they'd have told me about their back pains or their blood pressure.

My life with the Good Shepherd Sisters, an order which has served exploited and oppressed women from its first beginnings, has opened doors for me that otherwise would have remained locked. Women were willing to share their stories with me because I am a Good Shepherd Sister. Because of that I want to be sure I am not misunderstood about the path I believe the sexually abused need to travel before they can truly begin to live again.

One reason I wanted to share these women's stories is to offer hope to others who have had similar experiences. That doesn't mean they need to "get religion" or that they can't "be saved" without it. I know that for some women, organized religion has been more of a hindrance than a help.

Some have turned to ministers or priests—or nuns—and been rebuffed, misunderstood or blamed.

Some have been sexually abused by "upstanding" church members.

Some cannot believe in a loving God because their lives have been filled with so much pain.

The young woman who came to a Good Shepherd Home did not succeed because of religion. She succeeded because, for the first time in her life, she experienced unconditional love. A Sister loved that girl no matter what had happened to her or what she did. Often it took that young woman months, years, or even decades, to realize there was someone who loved her with no strings attached. That was the key that opened her heart. That was how she learned to begin to love herself.

Religion is supposed to help us experience a God who loves us unconditionally. But, unfortunately, it's not unusual that individuals of a particular denomination are unable to convey that message. All religions are made up of human beings and human beings make mistakes. The cardinal rule of Sister Euphrasia, founder of the Good Shepherd Sisters, was not "Baptize them." She asked us Sisters to make real, to make

personal, the untiring love of the Good Shepherd to each individual who comes into our lives. Sister Euphrasia wanted us
to love not ten girls at a time, but each girl, one by one, taking
her individual differences and needs into account.

I believe that when a person experiences unconditional
love, she is experiencing God. In his epistle, St. John put it
very simply: "God is love." Christ's commandment was "Love
others as you love yourself." But the victim of sexual abuse
must learn to love herself first. Not in a selfish way, but in a
way that says "I am a special individual. I was made to love
and be loved." But she can do neither until she experiences a
true love, a selfless love, a love that is freely given just because she is special, because she was made to be loved and to
love.

My own experience with love has always been rooted in my
faith. Or, to be more accurate, my faith has always been
rooted in love. I know I've been what some might call lucky
and others would call blessed. The semantics don't concern
me much. The knowledge that some women may be without
hope does.

The victim of sexual abuse does not need her name written
on the roster of a church or parish. She needs it inscribed in
the heart of a fellow human being.

She needs to be loved. Just like all of us.

Such love *can* be found: in individual therapy, in support
groups, in residential treatment centers, in play therapy for
very young children, in marriage, in family, with friends.

We began with Rosemary's story. This is the conclusion.

After graduation I took a room in the home of a little old
lady who had a will of iron and a heart of gold. She was lonely
and frightened; mostly, I think, because she didn't hear well.

I worked for her whenever my regular job allowed me free
time. For the first six months I didn't like living there. She
seemed to think I was bad and needed watching. I tried to do
all I could for her.

Again and again I went back to see Sister Gertrude and
pour out all my grief. She would smile and not say much. I
finally took the hint: I had to face my own problems.

Actually, I had made many close friends with the Sisters. I
used to phone Sister Raphael every other day because I really
missed her. She encouraged me in so many ways. I returned
often to the Home to take part in many of the social activities
and to see the movies with the girls. For the first three
months after I left, in fact, I spent all Sunday, every Sunday,
at the Home. Gradually and slowly, I broke that, trying to develop friendships outside of the Home and the Sisters and the
girls. Besides, I was getting pretty fond of a certain young
man.

He asked me to go steady, and I agreed. All that ended
when he asked me to marry him. I said yes at first, but then
he got in a hurry and that scared me off. What's worse, he
wouldn't leave me alone after that. He kept calling on the
phone, and practically drove me crazy. I swore off men.

Not for too long, however.

I began seeing another young man, but only during the
day. He was nice, and I was careful.

Then came the day my life changed. A young sailor came
into the drug store where I was working, and bought a box of
candy. I started to wrap it, only to find myself staring at him
and tearing the paper. He kept looking at me. Finally he said,
"You've torn the paper. Will you wrap it again."

That made me angry. "I suppose you want this for some
girl?"

"As a matter of fact, I do."

I threw the box at him. "Wrap it yourself," I said.

He left, and he took a part of me with him.

He actually phoned me later. Again and again. I took him out to the Sisters to meet them; they were my family, and I needed to know whether they approved. They liked him, too.

Finally the war ended. Everyone was so happy and thankful. The day after that I got a long-distance call. Would I marry him?

Would I!

I immediately rushed out to the Home to share my good news. Finally the day came. The Sisters prepared our wedding breakfast at the Home, and they served us. All of the Sisters came to congratulate us. We got gifts and good wishes. The next day we left for our honeymoon.

I asked Rosemary to look back and describe the problems she had had as a teenager, and tell about their cause. She wrote:

What made me react the way I did? Because of being fooled, lied to, and used for others' amusement. I finally decided that everybody was out to use me for their own ends. Again and again a person who had been my friend would suddenly turn away and have no further use for me. I grew up in this atmosphere of mistrust and suspicion. All the people I knew said that I was no good then and never would be. This hurt, and I set out to prove that they were wrong. I built a wall around myself for my own safety, and I became reserved. Then people thought I was stuck-up. But I was really covering up my own insecurity and aloneness so people couldn't shove me around. If anybody corrected me, I took that as a challenge to show that person that he or she was wrong. I *had* to believe in myself because nobody else did.

Almost forty years have passed since Rosemary left the Good Shepherd Home. To find out what has happened in the intervening years I traveled to meet with her.

She is the same Rosemary: forthright, frank, loving, proud of her husband and children.

Rosemary has six children and twenty-four grandchildren.

She told me how much she had loved school and had longed for an education. She had won a scholarship to a four-year college while at the Good Shepherd Home. She recalled how hard it had been to give that up, marry the man she loved, and watch him get through college on the G-I Bill. She has encouraged her husband to continue his education whenever possible; his framed diplomas attest to that encouragement.

Rosemary made sure that her children graduated from high school; some have gone to college or to professional school, and all are making certain that their children get the best possible education. One granddaughter has just won a scholarship for modeling school. I couldn't write fast enough to keep up with the scholarships and the continued studies.

Rosemary lives in a beautiful home in an exclusive suburb. With tremendous pride, she showed me the patio she and her husband had built, the yard they had landscaped, the wallpaper she and a daughter had hung, the inlaid wood treasures she and her husband brought back from the European country where he had been sent as an executive of his company.

She talked about her love of God and the peace she has always found in God's personal love for her. Her entire demeanor and bearing speak of peace.

And yet.

Over and over I heard the words, "I always felt so useless; I never thought I could do anything. I don't know where the feeling comes from."

Talking to Rosemary without sensing her intelligence is impossible. But she was surprised to learn that she could build the patio with her husband, amazed to discover her skills with interior decorating.

And I still heard the anger. "Forgiving does not mean forgetting," she said simply. "I can't forget. I'm always vigilant."

I watched over my girls. I told them never to climb on Grandpa's lap or let him hold them because he had a bad heart. I didn't want to frighten them; they never knew what he did. I wanted them to love their grandfather. But I watched him.

Any questions my children asked about sex, I always answered, honestly and openly. I would not let them encounter danger because they were not informed.

When my girls married, they were virgins. I'm proud of that.

I have never told any of my relatives about the incest. To this day, they think I had an illegitimate child, and that's why I went away. Because of that belief, they turned their backs on me all of my married life.

When I left home, my brother was five. Today he's fifty-seven. He still cannot understand why I left him at so young an age to go away to school. I will never explain.

All of my married life, I have felt angry.

But I made up my mind that what happened would not ruin my life nor my family's. I told my husband what happened; he is the only person besides the Good Shepherd Sisters who knows. God has forgiven me for my sins; as God forgave, so do I.

But I can't forget. It's all as vivid to me today as the day it first began.

I'll never forget the social worker I first talked to; I ran away just so I could talk to a woman social worker. It's not like today. She would not believe me. She said I couldn't accept discipline. I was a bad girl, no parent could do such a thing.

I said I'd undergo whatever tests she wanted. Then when they believed me, and I discovered that my dad would go to jail, I lied. I had to lie. I loved my dad, as Dad. He could have put us all in the orphanage when my mother died so young, but he worked and kept us together. It was a horrendous decision.

I can still cry about it. I'm still embarrassed because I love him.

When my dad was dying, we had moved several states away. We went back. But he was in a coma. I called his name. He came out of it. He couldn't speak, but he looked at me, and the tears came. I had waited all my life for him to apologize, to ask for forgiveness; I think he asked it then, and I forgave him.

I used to have nightmares sometimes, and wake up beating my husband off, thinking it was my father. That only happened when I got a letter from home, or got some news of him. After his death, all of that was over.

I have always had a very simple faith, always believed that God would take care of me. Now when I go to bed with my husband there are no ghosts. I have become a different person, and he is a different person. Our marriage has always been, and is, good.

I was determined that what had happened was not going to spoil our life. It has not.

And yet, the whole thing is as vivid in my mind as it was then; when one is hurt that badly, the hurt remains. I have put it in a compartment in my life, and moved on.

Life is for living. All that I have lived is a part of me. But I am not bitter.

Very simply, I have moved on.

Rosemary has moved on through life, but always with a struggle. Nevertheless, she has become a beautiful person and a successful wife and mother.

Some of us get diabetes, and learn to live with that handicap, some have poor eyesight, and others have an enduring weight problem. We can go through life feeling sorry for ourselves and trying to win sympathy, or we can accept that wounded part of ourselves, and move on.

Rosemary has never totally recovered from the deep and abiding angers of her teenage years. The next young woman whose victory I am going to recount has struggled intermittently with a pervasive fear of sexual relations with her husband. Nevertheless, she has talked with her husband about her problem, and she, like Rosemary, is moving on.

Marcie has recounted the story of her abuse at home, and the further abuse she suffered from the legal system.

In the Good Shepherd Home I found a friend, Sister Victoria.

She cared and understood. At times I felt as though she were the only person in the whole world who had ever cared, ever understood. I would go into her office and cry and talk. Or just sit and cry for hours at a time. She wouldn't say a word, just listened and loved me. She loved me for who I was. She didn't care what had happened.

Sister Victoria is a Good Shepherd Sister. That was a new world to me. I had never known any nuns. I had never known a loving caring woman, either.

I told her how I hated my parents, and I needed to say that many times over. Sister was never too busy, never had other things to do. She was there for me.

I had hated going to the Good Shepherd Home, but ended up staying past the time required, even well on into college. And I loved Sister Victoria.

I never got anything out of the Catholic service on Sundays. A wonderful minister and his wife also came on Sundays for Protestant services. I got a lot out of that. The minister and his wife often took me into their home for weekends.

Their son was a handsome hunk, and I fell in love with him. He was a year older than I. Sister let me go out on dates, and then he proposed, but several months later he broke the engagement; I was ready to die of a broken heart, but we were too young then for a commitment, and he was right.

After two years of college I became a licensed practical nurse, and went to work.

Sister and the minister and his wife had given me so much love that I thought my problems were over.

I belong to the Church of God of Prophecy. Every year our church has a retreat. I was excited about going and, at this point, felt good about myself. One speaker brought up sex abuse and talked about inner healing, inviting those of us who had been abused at home to seek that healing.

By her words, she drew out all my feelings, and the gnawing resentment still seething far below the surface. I still ached with the pain. The speaker recalled God's unconditional love for us and urged that we accept that love.

But even though I realized that I must deal with that residue of pain, I thought that not even God could get rid of all my hurt. I told God that I could not believe that he could heal me: "It's too much," I told him. "I've never forgotten or forgiven. The job is too big even for you. But I'll give it a try."

I went to a retreat counselor. "Let's go over it year by year," she suggested, "and ask the Lord to wash it away, and take the hurt and bitterness out." And we did, year by year, from age nine through thirteen. After that experience I felt like a new person, and wanted to contact my parents.

I told my mother that I wished us to be friends, although I could never relate to her as my mother. We dealt with the hurt and the anger, admitted our sins to each other, and forgave, and got rid of the whole horrid thing. She, too, had been an abused child, and had simply passed on the hurt.

Then I turned to my father, whom I had really loved. That childhood love had made the pain and sense of betrayal even worse. My dad and I talked for hours. I discovered that he had never been able to forgive himself for what he had done to me, and that he, too, needed healing.

We forgave each other and still kept the love between us. I adore my father. And, of course, I have come to realize that he was getting no sexual satisfaction from his wife—but it was still wrong of him to come to me, and to whip me all the times he did. My relationship with my father now is the kind of father-daughter relationship which I wish I might have had as a child.

They say a girl tends to marry a man like dear old dad, and I did. Matthew is quiet, physically strong, domineering, but in an entirely different way, and a very hard worker. He provides our monthly check, and he does it well.

We spent one weekend on a Christian couples retreat. The talks dealt with marriage commitment and personal relationship. That's when I fell totally in love with Matthew.

My father gave me away. He remarried, and my step-mother is a jewel, a real mother to me. My own mother did not come, but that didn't matter.

Matthew and I have been married eight and a half years now, and we did go through one rocky time—because of the adjustments I had to make.

Initially, every bride is on Cloud Nine and I was no exception. But on my wedding night I was scared to death, scared to let Matthew touch me, and scared to tell him why. Anyhow, I went through with it. He fell asleep and I lay awake and cried.

I loved Matthew dearly, but for the first few months, I cringed every time he got affectionate. I dreaded making love. The desire was there, but not the mechanics.

Finally Matthew asked, "Don't you want me to make love to you?"

I wanted him to kiss and hug me, but I had put up an unconscious barrier against sex.

"Have I hurt you?" he asked me.

"No," I said, "not at all.

"Matthew, this is really hard for me, but I have to talk to you. Listen, please, and don't talk."

Then I told him of the sexual abuse, how I hated it, got punished for it, was never allowed to talk about sex, never had anything explained to me until, finally, it was conveyed in street talk. "I learned that sex is dirty and shameful," I explained. "Sex is good and beautiful. I know that in my head, but not in my body.

"I'm in love with you and I want this marriage to work. Please be patient with me, please treat me gently and softly. I don't want sex to be a problem, but sometimes it is.

"When the problem times come, please be with me, helping me to work it through."

Marcie and Matthew, together, have created a lovely marriage for themselves, a nice home, and two beautiful children.
Marcie plans to be a registered nurse some day; for now, she
wants to stay at home and enjoy her children and her quiet
life, free from turmoil and fear. Occasionally she still does
have some difficulty with sex, but she talks that out with
Matthew. Possibly she will always experience some problem
with sex, but she won't let that handicap cripple her.

Marcie has moved on.

All seemed well with Angela. She had graduated from high
school and moved out on her own. She had, she thought,
worked out her problems during her time with the Good
Shepherd Home.

And then her father was killed.

In the lightning flash of his death Angela discovered that
she was once more rootless. In fact, she had never trusted
anybody else but her father, despite her efforts to form relationships.

Personal relationships are one of the biggest challenges fac-
ing the sexually abused child at home. A person she had loved
and trusted had betrayed her. She is reluctant to love and
trust somebody else.

Angela had more difficulties in this area than anybody else
because it was her father who had betrayed her, but her dad
was all she had.

I was in shock. Sister knew that. She invited me to stay for a

few days, gave me cleaning work, and paid me for it. I was so
scared I hardly stepped out of the door. The few days turned
into a few months. I talked and talked to Sister. At long last I
came to really love her, really appreciate her love. I put down
roots.

Eventually I found work and went to business college for
two years. In May I was elected the May Queen at the college. I was thrilled.

During that period when I had been, literally, on the ropes,
I had been writing down goals and the steps needed to attain
them. Now some money came through, left by my father, so I
bought my own printing shop and became self-employed. The
Home's executive director co-signed for a car for me; I established credit, and I prayed. And I joined the middle class.

"Pray for healing of memories," Sister would say. I tried.
But I still find myself tripping up on situations which others
mastered in childhood. Just belonging to a real family with my
husband, two children, and my in-laws takes effort on my
part. The formation of real relationships will always be a challenging task, I'm sure. My husband is patient with me, and I
try.

It's important for people to realize that change in one's life
is okay. Most of us think that our lives should be like somebody else's. But God has called us each by name, each to be
her own person. Each of us needs to develop faith in herself.
And each of us needs guidance.

When I feel completely dumb, deaf, and blind, I hang on to
scripture. I read and recall it, and know that it speaks to me,
here and now.

I've had to fight for life, struggle to survive, attack first before I get run over. I've had to be wild.

That determination to hang on, even when I could find

nothing to hang on to; to develop aggressive self-determination; to fight a stubborn, teeth-gritted battle with the forces determined to destroy me, came to me from God.

Now I'm on the Board of Directors of the Good Shepherd Home, the same Home where, once, I could not get out of the Yellow Cottage.

Me!

I made it!

Occasionally a sexually abused child at home comes into womanhood and maturity without visible scars. That can happen, but it does not happen frequently.

Iris graduated from high school in the Good Shepherd Home and walked out into the world. She had already taken a lot of responsibility in the Home, and had been holding a part-time job.

Because she still clung to a fragment of hope that her family might be as she wished instead of as she had suffered from, her first venture was to move back into the family circle.

Almost eighteen when I left the Home, I went to live with an aunt. I was very much aware of three things: I loved the Sisters, I cared about my school, and I felt very proud of my accomplishments. Adjustment to my new environment was not really a problem, but I wanted to belong to a family. With my own family, the old wounds were again re-opened. Nine months later, unhappy and floundering, I walked away from old family ties forever.

I enlisted in the Marine Corps and loved it. I took every opportunity for travel and study. Eventually I met a young naval officer, a hospital administrator, and we have been happily married for twenty-nine years. He has been an excellent provider, loving, caring and supportive, even though his military career has brought many disruptions, long months and years of separation and lonely responsibility. But I adapted to and enjoyed this hectic lifestyle. I have always participated and responded to needs where they exist: to direct a church choir, teach over two hundred youths how to bowl, coordinate community endeavors, counsel young marrieds with financial troubles, conduct polls during elections, or edit a community newspaper. Throughout the years I have remained the moving force, the one to be depended upon, the creator of ideas, the home decorator, and above all, the wonderful seamstress, exactly as I had been at the Good Shepherd Home.

We have two healthy, productive and successful children who grew up in the '60s and '70s without ever once giving cause for shame or embarrassment. Our married son, twenty-seven, is a mortgage broker; our daughter, twenty-four, studied at the University of Madrid, graduated from an American university, and is following a bilingual career with an international satellite communications firm.

I looked up in the hospital records of the young stepbrother I was accused of "murdering." According to the records, I gave my stepbrother a simple paregoric; he died of a ruptured appendix and peritonitis. A couple of years ago I learned that my father had never wanted my brother and me and had, in fact, tried to give us away. He blamed my brother for my mother's death. If he had not been born, she would not have died. I had the misfortune of looking like her and served as a constant reminder. He didn't care what my stepmother did to us; he only wanted us out of his sight.

At forty-nine years old I am happy and consider myself extraordinarily fortunate. I never look back with bitterness or regret, only curiosity. From the Sisters I learned moral and ethical values which guided and governed not only my own life and family, but also those with whom I have come in contact. As a functioning, contributing, imperfect individual, I was, in a sense, born in the Good Shepherd Home. Because the Sisters loved me and cared, I love and care. It's as simple as that.

Finally we come to Pearl.

Pearl struggled through a terrible ordeal, and uncovered not only her own victimization, but that of her children. And then, as an anticlimax, the man who seduced her children countersued.

For myself, I have discovered that I am not crazy, and never was. Maybe it doesn't sound like it, but for me that discovery has been a Big Thing.

I decided to try taking a subject or two at a junior college. I doubted that I could pass or even learn anything, but I wanted to try.

After three years of that, I worked up enough courage and faith in myself to dare a transfer to a four-year college and allow myself to think about getting a degree.

For a whole lifetime I had thought I could never get a degree. But I did take the subjects, and my college grade average ran between 3.5 and 3.8.

I wanted a degree in social work. An internship was required. I decided to work with battered women at a neighborhood house. Then I was offered an internship at a Good Shepherd Sisters' shelter. When the internship ended, the Sisters invited me to join the shelter staff as an after-care worker.

I had never believed that I could actually find a job, not to mention holding one. How thrilled I am.

I love this work.

I went to a local hospital and learned how to lead rap sessions for sexually abused women. One of the Sisters and I have led several for the women here. I tell them my story. They often open up after that, and those who suffered that violation are able to talk about the childhood incest in their own lives.

All of our women were abused, either emotionally, physically, or sexually, or all three, in their own homes. That abuse may be the factor which set them up for battering and beating in their married lives. Until they become able to recognize and deal with the underlying unconscious mechanisms, they may never be able to change the tenor of their own lives.

In the shelter the Sisters help them do that. I give them the support they need in after-care.

Through most of the victories runs the thread of self-doubt. The child who is sexually abused at home believes, deep down, that something must be wrong with *her*. Somehow, she must be guilty. Her father, or whatever relative, being such a good man, could not have abused her unless she somehow made him do that. Even though she comes to know intellectually that she has been in no way culpable, the self-doubt clings tenaciously on.

I noted the self-doubt in every single woman except Iris. It struck me most forcefully in Rosemary. If anybody has achieved success, that person is Rosemary. She had won a four-year scholarship to college which she gave up so that her husband could get through school. Her children are successful in their individual lives. Her marriage is an unusually happy one. But I still heard her say, a couple of weeks ago,

"My husband and I built that patio between us; I never thought I could do anything like that. . . . I never thought, really, that I could do anything."

I stood there, looking at an attractive, happy, successful wife and mother, a person whom I would trust in any emergency, and could scarcely believe my ears: "I didn't think I could. . . ."

Vividly, once more, I was confronted with the lasting effects of childhood sexual abuse in the home.

But Rosemary had triumphed over those feelings, and had achieved in spite of them.

So have Marcie, and Angela, and Pearl, and Iris.

The sexually abused *can* overcome.

With my own eyes and in my own experience I have seen the proof lived out hundreds of times. On that fact I have predicated this book.

The sexually abused carry a handicap, but who among us does not?

The child sexually abused at home can triumph over the tragedy and can complete the footrace of life and win.

TWENTY

Coming in First

I REMEMBER the happy days I spent in school.

I remember school best of all, probably because most of my adult life has been spent in schools, always as the principal.

And I remember the school of my own childhood.

It was a one-room rural school close to Calgary, Alberta. My father taught there. Later on it became a two-room school, with my mother teaching too. After the division, I was still in my father's room.

My father was a gifted teacher. He taught grades five through high school in a German immigrant area. The children talked German at home, but they learned reading, writing, and arithmetic in English.

Examinations for the eighth grade and high school were made up by the Department of Education in Edmonton; they were also corrected and graded there. Even had there not been this external check on my father's work, his students would have mastered the subject matter.

My father taught the basics. He insisted on them. He taught students how to write good English compositions, and he demanded pages of memory work, both poetry and prose. He not only provided me with the best possible foundation for college, he developed in me a tenacious memory which is still one of my best assets.

As a school principal I structured my schools according to my father's example. When I transferred to the States, I was aghast at the much lower standards of American schools; most students in high school could not have made the eighth grade in my father's schoolroom. Consequently, I insisted on the acquisition of everyday skills. My schools might not have been exciting but students learned, and enjoyed doing it.

Most of all, perhaps, the girls appreciated the quiet atmosphere of the schoolroom. They had enjoyed precious little quiet in their lives, and they absorbed the silence.

Throughout the years, my students made their way into a variety of contests, and won most of them: speech, recitation, essays, photography, art. To my amazement, we encountered jealousy. I had supposed that everybody would be delighted when teenagers who were in some way handicapped rated first place. I was wrong.

In some locations it was made clear to me that good students from good schools ought to come in first.

All admire the graciousness with which Jesus welcomed those with special needs, and his visits to their dinners and homes. We like to think we can follow his teachings, but we don't expect *those people* to occupy the place of honor when we good folks attend.

The sexually abused child does have more urgent problems than education, but should education be neglected, the child is left to struggle with an additional handicap. Schools should be adapted to meet a child's educational needs, even when that child is hampered with emotional problems.

Emotional and behavioral problems can be triggered by a variety of factors, of which sexual abuse is only one. Since teachers are unlikely to know the source of their students' learning difficulties, we need schools adapted to all students.

We need, also, to re-involve high school dropouts.

Circumstances have combined to thrust Good Shepherd Sisters into the forefront of innovative educational planning, although we never intended to become educators.

Throughout the years, as we have listened to teens tell of school situations which were a factor in their behavioral and/or emotional problems, Good Shepherd Sisters have developed several remedial educational models.

In some areas of the country, the Sisters have set up special education day schools, not for slow learners but for the emotionally and behaviorally handicapped. These schools are not limited to such students.

In one city, forty-eight school districts regularly avail themselves of a special education school administered by Good Shepherd Sisters; students are mainstreamed back into their own public schools as rapidly as feasible.

The Sisters have created schools for long-term dropouts. One of these schools aims at preparing students to pass their G.E.D., with the goal of further professional or college education, or full-time employment. Another guides dropouts through the curricula necessary for a high school diploma; half of these graduates have gone on to college, while the other half are working full time.

Another concept is the mini-school: a room in a public school for children who are burdened with learning problems caused by a variety of factors. The room is set up with specialists; classes are kept very small; breakfast and lunch are provided. These facilities, in either elementary or junior high schools, are organized and administered by Good Shepherd Sisters.

Each alternative school provides more counselors than are usually available. Often, each child is seen individually every week and is involved in weekly group therapy. Whenever a child needs help, that help is instantly available.

In one city Good Shepherd Sisters provide these kinds of services for many private elementary schools.

The question has recently arisen as to whether schools can or ought to provide some education on sexual abuse, and schools are increasingly adding this topic to their curriculum. When this effort brings sexual abuse in the home to the surface, the situation becomes controversial.

Sister Mary is the administrator of one alternative school which uses a constructive approach. In the context of a course on Contemporary Issues, one issue the class deals with is sexual abuse. Within such a framework some of the teenage boys and girls are relieved to be able to talk about their own painful experiences. The initial presentation of their problem is a heavy issue for the youngsters. Remarks such as, "I don't know why I am talking about this" are common.

Within the group and schoolroom framework, an understanding of the dynamics involved is imparted. So too is the relationship of abuser and victim. The tendency of an abused child to repeat that pattern in later life, and to do so endlessly, is underscored.

Should teenagers then express a need for individual therapy, an experienced staff counselor is available.

The recommendation for a child sexually abused in the home may be placement in a foster home, a group home, a psychiatric setting, her own home if the abuser is out of the community, or in a residential center.

For this problem, as for a variety of problems, residential treatment centers will seldom be recommended until all other possible options have been exhausted. Such a placement might be requested following psychiatric or other treatment, should the child's own home, a foster home, or a group home be seen as inappropriate for the child.

The shortcoming I am aware of in most residential treatment centers is the limited term of residence. Based on my own years of experience, in the short space of three or six months, youth who have been victimized are only beginning to develop that relationship of trust necessary for one-on-one treatment, but six months is sometimes as long a time as the child may stay. The bottom line is funding. But lack of adequate treatment for adolescents will end up costing a lot more money later on.

According to the April 1983 newsletter published by the National Coalition of American Nuns:

Incest is the most long-standing grievous offense against one-fifth to one-third of all girls 16 years of age and under. This criminal offense against girls and young women is one of the greatest single, unmentioned, unsolved, untreated and non-legislated-against abuses that exists today.

Statistics gathered from private and family therapists, sex clinics and clinicians, research reports and law enforcement agencies give these startling figures on incest and its results:

Fifty percent of incest crimes are committed against girls under the age of ten years. The youngest known victim is a five-month-old infant. . . .

The psychological and physical effects of incest extend far into adult life. For example, 92 percent of the adult women in alcoholic recovery therapy have suffered from incest; 70 percent of adolescent female drug addicts; and 75 percent of adolescent prostitutes were thus abused. Over 90 percent of the women in prison today were victims of incest attacks in childhood.

From these statistics the long-term cost to society can be deduced.

I have observed a few residential treatment centers for adolescents which offer treatment for as long as required, and do so very adequately.

Sister Ella has been engaged in child-care work for twenty-five years in four states. Most child-care workers are burned out long before they hit the twenty-five-year mark of service, but not Sister Ella. "Too many child-care workers take the responsibility for the youth themselves," she said. "I don't. I place the responsibility where it belongs: on the youth.

"They will be obliged to make their own decisions and chart their own course after they leave us. Unless they learn those skills now, they will be hard pressed to develop them after they have bidden us goodbye."

Each teenager goes out to school every day. Some students may have skipped more school in their lives than they attended. "How do you do it?" I asked.

"I phone their schools regularly, always attend parent-teacher conferences; and am always there when a student is rewarded for special achievement or is involved in a particular school celebration," Sister Ella said. "The girls know that.

"Study hours at night are regular and supervised. School is made a priority. A girl failing in school is campused until her grades improve."

Girls placed in this residence may remain until they turn twenty-one, if necessary. Having completed high school, they can attend college. Meanwhile, each is gradually prepared and eased into independent living until the young woman finds herself in her own apartment with no further supervision.

Now, as I draw close to the end of this book, I recall, by some trick of memory, that my father always taught me to come in first.

Strange.

I had never wanted to become a teacher, and certainly not a school principal. My objective in life always has been, and is, to become a contemplative.

When I was assigned to teaching, I would have preferred the challenge of teaching in the graduate school of a university. For years, I have pondered over those turns in my life.

Now, by some mental twist—not unlike hitting the right key on a word processor and watching jumbles of words straightening themselves out as though by magic—the crooked lines have bent straight.

But not until I tie in one more memory.

Many years ago I read in the diocesan paper of the city in which I was then principal, an invitation to all Catholic high schools to join in one huge graduation. Thus, said the article, the celebration would be bigger and better than any single school might offer.

That sounded good to me.

True, most of my students were not Catholic. But Good Shepherd Sisters administered and taught in the school. Therefore, I reasoned, we were invited.

I mailed in my application.

Good Shepherd girls, I was told, could not graduate with students from Catholic high schools.

I was appalled. While this attitude has almost disappeared, it was real then. Terribly real.

The last shall be the first, said the Lord.

When those final trumpet blasts sound and all of us line up at the pearly gates, I'm going to grab on to the school books of a high school dropout; clutch the miniskirts of a couple of prostitutes and the prison uniforms of a woman or two; gather up some plaster casts of the battered and beaten; and hang on to the case histories of hopeless psychiatric patients and the empty bottles of alcoholics.

And the Lord will say, "Come right in. I was in prison and you visited me, walking the dark streets alone and you cared, beaten up and you ministered, lying in the gutter and you loved, crippled by my problems and you taught me."

I'm going to smile, big, and link my arms with those of my friends who usually came in last, walk up to the front row in the heavenly mansion, and we will sit down together, my friends and I.

Notes

CHAPTER TWO: IN TROUBLE

Page
12   seldom reveal the sexual abuse: Banmen, John, "The incidence, treatment and counseling of incest," *International Journal for the Advancement of Counselling*, 1982, 5:2, 201–206. See also Rush, F., *The Best Kept Secret* (Engelwood: Prentice-Hall, 1980) 4–5.

13   an easier path for all of us: Brownmiller, S., *Against Our Will* (New York: Simon and Schuster, 1975) 281.

CHAPTER THREE: MARCIE

Page
15   My brother John began: Cole, Ellen, "Sibling incest: the myth of benign sibling incest," *Women and Therapy*, 1982, 1:3, 79–89.

CHAPTER FOUR: UNTIL WE SPEAK OUT

Page
22   ual assaults in their: Herman, J., *Father-Daughter Incest* (Cambridge: Harvard University Press, 1981) 1–9.

22   within their own homes: Linedecker, C. L., *Children in Chains* (New York: Everest, 1981) 93. "A study by a research

team at the University of Washington School of Medicine, Seattle, indicated that as many as nine out of ten instances of sexual abuse of children in this country are unreported to authorities."

23 and the children's protection movement: Finkelhor, D., *Child Sexual Abuse* (New York: The Free Press, 1984) 3.

23 especially fathers and stepfathers: Herman, J., "Recognition and treatment of incestuous families," *International Journal of Family Therapy*, 1983, 5:2, 81–91.

23 that 38 percent of these women: Russell, D. E., "Incidence and prevalence of intrafamilial and extrafamilial sexual abuse of female children," *Child Abuse and Neglect*, 1983, 7, 133–146.

23 out of forty abused by biological fathers: Russell, D. E., "The prevalence and seriousness of incestuous abuse: stepfathers vs biological fathers," *Child Abuse and Neglect*, 1984, 8:1, 15–22.

23 for 10 percent of all reported cases of childhood sexual abuse in the family: Goodwin, J.; Cormier, L.; Owen, J., "Grandfather-granddaughter incest: a trigenerational view," *Child Abuse and Neglect*, 1983, 7:2, 163–170.

23 are the abusers strangers: Conte, J. R., "Progress in treating the sexual abuse of children," *Social Work*, 1984, May–June, 258–262.

23 under the age of eighteen each year: Finkelhor, D., op. cit., 2.

24 the Child Sexual Abuse Treatment Program: Giaretto, H., "A comprehensive child sexual abuse treatment program," *Child Abuse and Neglect*, 1982, 6:3, 263–278.

24 molested in their homes each year: Stark, E., "The unspeakable family secret," *Psychology Today*, May 1984, 42.

24 to kill themselves: Ibid.

24 the average age of the first incident being eleven years old: Husain, A., and Chapel, J. L., "History of incest in girls admitted to a psychiatric hospital," *American Journal of Psychiatry*, 1983, 140:5, 591–593.

24 and that 18 percent admit to forcible rape: Abel, G., et al., "The characteristics of men who molest young children," presented at the World Congress of Behavior Therapy, Washington, D.C., 1983.

25 chooses to ignore incest, deny it: Taubman, S., "Incest in context," *Social Work*, 1984, 29:1, 35– 40.

26 had been sexually abused in childhood, too: Kasper, C. J., Baumann, R. C., Alford, J., "Sexual abusers of children: the lonely kids," *Transactional Analysis Journal*, 1984, 14:2, 131– 135.

26 one of the men would say: Farber, E. D., et al., "The sexual abuse of children: a comparison of male and female victims," *Journal of Clinical Child Psychology*, 1984, 13:3, 294– 297.

26 the case is thrown out of court: Stone, L.; Tyler, R., and Mead, J., "Law enforcement officers as investigators and therapists in child sexual abuse: a training model," *Child Abuse and Neglect*, 1984, 8, 75– 82.

27 Blaming the women was easier than believing them: Finkelhor, op. cit., 11. Herman, J., op. cit., Ch. 1. Masson, J., *The Assault on Truth: Freud's Suppression of the Seduction Theory* (New York: Farrar Straus Giroux, 1984.) McCarthy, B., "Incest and psychotherapy," *Irish Journal of Psychotherapy*, 1982, 9:1, 11– 16. Peters, J. J., "Children who are victims of sexual assault and the psychology of offenders," *American Journal of Psychotherapy*, 1976, 30:3, 398– 421. Rush, F., op. cit., 80– 104. Tavris, C., "How Freud betrayed women," *Ms.*, March 1984, 78– 80.

27 Alice Miller writes: Miller, A., *Thou Shalt not be Aware*, (New York: Farrar Straus Giroux, 1984.)

28 one textbook on basic psychiatry stated: Herman, J., op. cit. The book is *Comprehensive Textbook of Psychiatry*, 2nd ed. (Baltimore: Williams and Wilkins, 1975) 1532.

28 begins before puberty: O'Hare, J. and Taylor, K., "The reality of incest," *Women and therapy*, 1983, 2:2– 3, 215– 229.

31 a fatherly kiss: Finkelhor, D., op. cit., 18.

31 accusing me of lying: Carpenter, K. S., "Children's reliability in sex offense accusations," *Medical Aspects of Human Sexuality*, 1979. Rush, F., op. cit., 155– 156.

32 the long and difficult judicial procedure: Berliner, L. and Barbieri, M., "The testimony of the child victim of sexual assault," *Journal of Social Issues*, 1984, 40:2, 125– 137. Rush, F., op. cit., 155– 156. Weiss, E. H., "Incest accusation: assessing credibility," *Journal of Psychiatry and Law*, 1983, 11:3, 305– 317.

33   for keeping sexual abuse a secret: Tyler, A., and Brassard, M., "Abuse in the investigation and treatment of intrafamilial child sexual abuse," *Child Abuse and Neglect*, 1984, 8, 47–53.

33   her own guilt feelings are thus heightened: Stuart, J. and Greer, J., *Victims of Sexual Aggression* (New York: Van Nostrand, 1984) 61–73.

34   show several characteristics: Finkelhor, D., op. cit., 23–32; and *Sexually Victimized Children* (New York: Free Press, 1979.)

36   a willing cooperator in the abuse: Zuelzer, M. B., and Reposa, R. E. "Mothers in incestuous families," *International Journal of Family Therapy*, 1983, 5:2, 98–110.

37   in which one or both parents are alcoholics: Barnard, C. P., "Alcoholism and incest: improving diagnostic comprehensiveness," *International Journal of Family Therapy*, 1983, 5:2, 136–144.

37   abuse their children, sexually or physically: Taylor, R., "Marital therapy in the treatment of incest," *Social Casework*, 1984, 65:4, 195–202.

37   share histories of abuse in their families of origin: Wolf, S., "A multi-factor model of deviant sexuality." Talk given at the Third International Conference on Victimology, Lisbon, 1984.

37   abusing other children: Stuart, J. and Greer, J., *Victims of Sexual Aggression* (New York: Van Nostrand, 1984) 64.

38   therapy for problems in interpersonal relationships: Gaddini, R., "Incest as a developmental failure," *Child Abuse and Neglect*, 1983, 7:3, 357–358.

39   poorly prepared to perform the difficult task: Pierce, R. and Pierce L., "Analysis of sexual abuse hotline reports," *Child Abuse and Neglect*, 9:1, 37–45, 1985.

42   to have been *heterosexually* assaulted: Rush, F., op. cit., 181–182. Weisberg, D. K., *Children of the Night* (Lexington, KY: Lexington Books, 1985) 164–165: "For male youth whose first sexual experience was with a female, 66 percent of the youth were seduced by older females..."

42   Three psychologists found that: Meer, J., *Psychology Today*, Oct. 1984, 80.

42 Psychologist A. N. Groth: Stark, op. cit., 44. See also Fowler, C.; Burns, S.; and Roehl, J., "Counselling the incest offender," *International Journal of Family Therapy*, 1983, 5:2, 92–97.

45 hit the city streets: Rush, F., op. cit., 158–169.

CHAPTER SIX: "I FEEL OLD"

Page
54 may suffer serious personality damage: Finkelhor, D., op. cit., 15.

55 A recent study conducted at the New York State Psychiatric Institute: *The News and Observer*, Raleigh, NC, Feb. 17, 1985, 4C.

55 Suicide attempts. . . . : Bagley, C., "Mental health and the infamly sexual abuse of children and adolescents," *Canada's Mental Health*, 1984, 32:2, 19. See also Weisberg, D. K., op. cit., 116–120.

56 one of them may be successful: ibid., 116–117.

60 for which her relationship with her father: *The News and Observer*, Raleigh, NC, loc. cit.

61 victims of sexual assault in childhood: Walker, L., *The Battered Woman Syndrome* (New York: Springer, 1984) 20–21; 149; 164–165.

61 the learned helplessness: Gellen, M. I.; Hoffman, R. A.; Jones, M; Stone, M., "Abused and nonabused women: MMPI profile differences," *Personnel and Guidance Journal*, 1984, 62:10, 601–604. See also Walker, L., op. cit., 121–128.

65 many alcoholic women: Wilsnack, S. and Beckman, L., *Alcohol Problems in Women* (New York: Guilford Press, 1984) 203–205, 214, 216.

74 mixing pills with alcohol: Linedecker, C. L., *Children in Chains* (New York: Everest House, 1981) 90–91.

74–75 and become socially deviant: loc. cit.

CHAPTER EIGHT: CORNERS ARE SAFE

Page
95 to hope only meant to invite disappointment: Cf. Gaylin, W., *The Rage Within* (New York: Simon and Schuster, 1984).

CHAPTER TWELVE: STREET KIDS

Page

131 when she was eleven: Weisberg, D. K., op. cit., 170–171.

134 with the assistance they need: ibid., 229–261.

CHAPTER FOURTEEN: IN THE BUSINESS

Page

145 were sexually abused in childhood: McClory, R., "Freelance lay missionary brings hope to the hopeless," *National Catholic Reporter,* Kansas City, MO,Oct. 1984.

145 vast majority had been victims: Silbert, M. H. and Pines, A. M., "Early sexual exploitation as an influence on prostitution," *Social Work,* 1983, 28:285–289.

145 into those kinds of sexual services: Weisberg, D. K., op. cit., 95–96.

145 In San Francisco in 1977: Silbert, M. H., and Pines, A. M., "Entrance into prostitution," *Youth and Society,* June 1982, 471–500.

CHAPTER FIFTEEN: JENNY AND PATSY

Page

154 abusing her when she was six years old: Linedecker, C. L., op. cit., 91.

156 and we had sexuality groups: See Stuart, I. and Greer, J., op. cit., "Suggested Format for a Six-session Therapy Group," 118–123.

CHAPTER SEVENTEEN: LYNN

Page

165 Her husband beat her: Cf. Walker, L., op. cit., 142.

CHAPTER EIGHTEEN: RAISING CHILDREN WHO TELL

Page

171 raise children who tell: Finkelhor, D., op. cit., 98–149. Also Sanford, L., *The Silent Children* (New York: Anchor Press, 1980) 1–67.

CHAPTER NINETEEN: MOVING ON

Page

181   in individual therapy: Faria, G., and Belohlavek, N., "Treating female adult survivors in incest," *Social Casework*, 1984, 65:8, 465–471.

181   in support groups: Herman, J., and Schatzow, E., "Time-limited group therapy for women with a history of incest," *International Journal of Group Psychotherapy*, 1984, 34:4, 605–616.

CHAPTER TWENTY: COMING IN FIRST

Page

201   some education on sexual abuse: Finkelhor, D., op. cit., 147.

203   incest attacks in childhood: *NCAN News*, 1983, 13:2, 2.

Bibliography

ABUSER WITH SEVERAL, NOT ONE, VICTIM

Stark, E., "The Unspeakable Family Secret," *Psychology Today*, May 1984, 42–48.

ADULT SEXUAL ABUSE OF CHILDREN

Cook, M., and Howells, K., eds., *Adult Sexual Interest in Children*, New York: Academic Press, 1981.

ALCOHOL AND ABUSE

Vaillant, G. E., *The Natural History of Alcoholism*, Cambridge: Harvard University Press, 1983.

ANGER

Gaylin, W., *The Rage Within*, New York: Simon and Schuster, 1984.

BATTERED WOMEN

Walker, L., *The Battered Woman Syndrome*, New York: Springer Publications, 1984.

BROTHER–SISTER INCEST IGNORED

Dear Abby, "Mom Ignores Risk of Sibling Incest," *Seattle Times*, November 12, 1984.

CHILD BLAMED FOR TELLING

Berliner, Lucy, "Child Sexual Abuse: What Happens Next?" *Victimology*, 1977, 2, 327–331.

CHILD CRISIS LINE

Ney, P. G., Johnston, I. D., and Herron, J. L., "Social and Legal Ramifications of a Child Crisis Line." *Child Abuse and Neglect*, 1985, 9, 47–55.

CHILD UNLIKELY TO GET UNDERSTANDING

Summit, R. C., "The Child Sexual Abuse Accommodation Syndrome," *Child Abuse and Neglect*, 1983, 7, 177–193.

CHILDREN WHO DON'T TELL

Bass, Ellen, *I Never Told Anyone*, New York: Harper and Row, 1983.

COURT APPEARANCES

Berliner, Lucy, and Barbieri, M. K., "The Testimony of the Child Victim of Sexual Assault," *Journal of Social Issues*, 1984, 40:2, 125–137.
Conte, J. R., "Progress in Treating the Sexual Abuse of Children," *Social Work*, May–June 1984, 258–263.

EFFECTS OF SEXUAL ABUSE

Depression

"The Hurt that Keeps on Hurting," Help section, *Psychology Today*, November 1984, 74.

How Entire Family is Affected

Tyler, A. H., and Brassard, M. R., "Abuse in the Investigation and Treatment of Intrafamilial Child Sexual Abuse," *Child Abuse and Neglect*, 1984, 8, 47–53.

Long-lasting effects

Sawyer, S. G., "Dirty Little Secret of Incest Keeps Hurting for Years," *Raleigh* (NC) *News and Observer*, February 17, 1985.

FREUD

Finkelhor, David, *Child Sexual Abuse*, New York: The Free Press, 1984.
Herman, J. L., *Father-Daughter Incest*, Cambridge: Harvard University Press, 1981.
Masson, Jeffrey, *The Assault on Truth, Freud's Suppression of the Seduction Theory*, New York: Farrar, Straus, Giroux, 1984.
Miller, Alice, *Thou Shalt Not Be Aware*, New York: Farrar, Straus, Giroux, 1984.
Peters, Joseph J., "Children Who are Victims of Sexual Assault and the Psychology of Offenders," *American Journal of Psychotherapy*, 1976, 30:3, 398–421.
Tavris, C., "How Freud Betrayed Women," *Ms.*, March 1984, 78–80.

Bibliography

217

GENERAL

Allen, C., *Daddy's Girl*, New York: Wyndham Books, 1980.

Bixler, R., The Multiple Meanings of 'Incest,'" *Journal of Sex Research*, 1983, 19, 197–201.

Davidson, H. A., "Sexual Exploitation of Children: An Overview of Its Scope, Impact, and Legal Ramifications," *FBI Law Enforcement Bulletin*, 1984, 53:2, 26–31.

Giarreto, H., *Integrated Treatment of Child Sexual Abuse: Treatment and Training Manual*, Palo Alto, CA: Science and Behavior Books, 1982.

Goodwin, J., McCarthy, T., and DiVasto, P., "Prior Incest in Mothers of Abused Children," *Child Abuse and Neglect*, 1981, 5, 87–95.

Gordon, L., and O'Keefe, P., "Incest as a Form of Family Violence: Evidence from Historical Case Records," *Journal of Marriage and the Family*, February 1984, 46:1, 27–34.

List, S., *Forgiving*, New York: Dutton, 1982.

Martin, L., and Haddad, J., *We Have a Secret*, Newport Beach, CA: Crown Summit Books, 1982.

Renvoize, J., *Incest*, London: Routledge and Kegan Paul, 1982.

Ricks, C., *Carol's Story: The Sin Nobody Talks About*, Wheaton, IL: Tyndale House, 1982.

Rush, F., *The Best Kept Secret*, Englewood Cliffs, NJ: Prentice Hall, 1980.

Sanford, L., *The Silent Children. A Parent's Guide to the Prevention of Child Sexual Abuse*, New York: Anchor Press, 1980.

GRANDFATHER AS ABUSER

Goodwin, Jean, Cormier, L., and Owen, J., "Grandfather-granddaughter Incest: a Trigenerational View," *Child Abuse and Neglect*, 1983, 7:2, 163–170.

HELP FOR PARENTS

Kempe, R. and H., *The Common Secret: Sexual Abuse of Children and Adolescents*, New York: Freeman and Co., 1984.

Sanford, L., *The Silent Children*, New York: Doubleday, 1980

LAW AND SEXUAL ABUSE

Bulkley, J., *Child Sexual Abuse and the Law*, Washington, D.C.: American Bar Association, 1984.

―――― *Innovations in Prosecution of Child Sexual Abuse Cases*, Washington, D.C.: American Bar Association, 1981.

Conte, J., and Berliner, L., "Prosecution of the Offender in Cases of Sexual Assault against Children," *Victimology*, 1983, 8, 102–109.

―――― "Sexual Abuse of Children: Implications for Practice," *Social Casework*, 1981, 62:10, 601–606.

LONG-TERM TREATMENT NEEDED

Bagley, Chris, "Mental Health and the In-family Sexual Abuse of Children and Adolescents," *Canada's Mental Health*, 1984, 32:2, 17–22.

MALE SEX OFFENDERS

Butler, S., *Conspiracy of Silence: The Trauma of Incest*, New Glide Publications, 1978.

Carter, D., "At Center, Child Molesters are Treated as Addicts," *Seattle Post-Intelligencer*, April 2, 1985, Section C.

Groth, A., Hobson, W., and Gary, T., *The Child Molester—Clinical Observations*, New York: Hawthorne Press, 1980.

Herman, J. L., *Father-Daughter Incest*, Cambridge: Harvard University Press, 1981.

Lewis, D. D., Shankok, S. S., and Pincus, J. H., "Juvenile Male Sexual Assaulters," *American Journal of Psychiatry*, 1979, 136:9, 1194–1196.

Monahan, J., *The Clinical Prediction of Violent Behavior*, Rockville, MD: Department of Health and Human Services, 1980, 81–921.

Wolf, Steven, C., "Evaluation and Treatment of the Sexual Offender," manual published by the Sexual Assault Center, Harborview Medical Center, Seattle, WA 98104.

——— "A Multi-factor Model of Deviant Sexuality," paper presented at Third International Conference on Victimology, Lisbon, November 1984.

Wooden, W. S., and Parker, J., *Men Behind Bars*, New York: Plenum, 1984.

POLICE EDUCATION

Stone, L. E., Tyler, R. P., and Mead, J. J., "Law Enforcement Officers as Investigators and Therapists in Child Sexual Abuse: A Training Model," *Child Abuse and Neglect*, 1984, 8, 75–82.

PROSTITUTES

McLeod, Eileen, *Women Working: Prostitution Now*, London: Croom Helm, 1982.

McClory, R. J., "Freelance Lay Missionary Brings Hope to the Hopeless," *National Catholic Reporter*, Kansas City, MO, Oct. 5, 1984.

Rosen, R., *The Lost Sisterhood*, Baltimore: Johns Hopkins University Press, 1982.

PSYCHIATRIC HOSPITAL AND INCEST VICTIMS

Husain, A., and Chapel, J. L., "History of Incest in Girls Admitted to a Psychiatric Hospital," *The American Journal of Psychiatry*, 1983, 14015, 591–593.

SAFETY RULES FOR CHILDREN AND ADOLESCENTS

Bassett, C., *My Very Own Special Body Book*, Redding, CA: Hawthorne Press, 1981.

Bibliography 219

Committee for Children, *What Our Kids Don't Know Can Hurt Them,* 172 20th Ave., Seattle, WA 98122.

Fay, J., *He Told Me Not to Tell,* Renton, WA: King County Rape Relief, 1979.

Mackay, G., *Bubbylonian Encounter,* Topeka: Theater for Young America, Inc. (Available as theater script or videotape.)

Williams, J., *Once I Was a Little Bit Frightened,* P.O. Box 1655, Fargo, ND: Rape and Abuse Crisis Center, 1980.

——— *Green Light, Green Light People,* P.O. Box 1655, Fargo, ND: Rape and Abuse Crisis Center.

SALLY'S STORY

Johnson, M. K., and Foley, M. A., "Differentiating Fact from Fantasy: The Reliability of Children's Memory," *Journal of Social Issues,* 40:2, 33–50.

SCHOOL PROGRAMS TO HELP PREVENT CHILDHOOD SEX ABUSE

Brassard, M. R., Taylor, A. H., and Kehle, T. J., "School Programs to Prevent Intrafamilial Child Sexual Abuse," *Child Abuse and Neglect,* 1983, 7:2, 241–245.

SELF-HATE, SELF-MUTILATION, AND SUICIDE

Bagley, Chris, "Mental Health and the In-Family Sexual Abuse of Children and Adolescents," *Canada's Mental Health,* 1984, 32:2, 17–22.

Summit, R. C., "The Child Sexual Abuse Accommodation Syndrome," *Child Abuse and Neglect,* 1983, 7, 177–193.

SEXUALLY TRANSMITTED DISEASES IN CHILDREN

Logan, J., "Venereal Disease: Chilling Side Effect of Child Abuse, *The Philadelphia Inquirer,* November 20, 1984, Section F.

Price, J., and Forish, J., *The VD Book,* New York: Holt, Rinehart and Winston, 1976.

STATISTICS

American Humane Association, *The National Study on Child Neglect and Abuse Reporting,* Denver: AHA, 1982.

Conte, J. R., "Progress in Treating the Sexual Abuse of Children," *Social Work,* May–June 1984, 253–283.

Finkelhor, David, *Child Sexual Abuse,* New York: The Free Press, 1984.

——— "How Widespread Is Child Sexual Abuse?" *Children Today,* July–August 1984, 18–20.

National Coalition of American Nuns, *NCAN News,* April 1985, 13:2.

Russell, Diana E. H., "The Incidence and Prevalence of Intrafamilial and Extrafamilial Sexual Abuse of Female Children," *Child Abuse and Neglect,* 1983, 7:2, 133–146.

—— "The Prevalence and Seriousness of Incestuous Abuse: Stepfathers vs. Biological Fathers," *Child Abuse and Neglect*, 1984, 8:1, 15–22.

Sarafine, E., "An Estimate of Nationwide Incidence of Sexual Offenses Against Children," *Child Welfare*, 1979, 58, 127–134.

TRENDS AND PATTERNS OF THE SEXUAL ABUSE OF CHILDREN

Rogers, C., and Thomas, J., "Sexual Victimization of Children in the U.S.A.: Patterns and Trends," paper presented at Fourth International Congress on Child Abuse and Neglect, Paris, September 1982.

Index

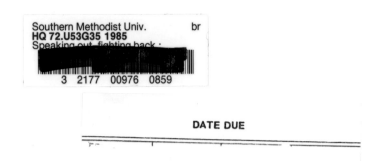
DATE DUE